Essays and Studies 1996

The English Association

The objects of the English Association are to promote the knowledge and appreciation of the English language and its literature, and to foster good practice in its teaching and learning at all levels.

The Association pursues these aims by creating opportunities of co-operation among all those interested in English; by furthering the recognition of English as essential in education; by discussing methods of English teaching; by holding lectures, conferences, and other meetings; by publishing journals, books, and leaflets; and by forming local branches.

Publications

The Year's Work in English Studies. An annual bibliography. Published by Blackwell.

The Year's Work in Critical and Cultural Theory. An annual bibliography. Published by Blackwell.

Essays and Studies. An annual volume of essays by various scholars assembled by the collector covering usually a wide range of subjects and authors from the medieval to the modern. Published by D.S. Brewer.

English. A journal of the Association, *English* is published three times a year by the Association.

The Use of English. A journal of the Association. *The Use of English* is published three times a year by the Association.

Newsletter. A *Newsletter* is published three times a year giving information about forthcoming publications, conferences, and other matters of interest.

Benefits of Membership

Institutional Membership
Full members receive copies of *The Year's Work in English Studies*, *Essays and Studies*, *English* (3 issues) and three *Newsletters*.

Ordinary Membership covers *English* (3 issues) and three *Newsletters*.

Schools Membership includes copies of each issue of *English* and *The Use of English*, one copy of *Essays and Studies*, thee *Newsletters*, and preferential booking and rates for various conferences held by the Association.

Individual Membership
Individuals take out Basic Membership, which entitles them to buy all regular publications of the English Association at a discounted price, and attend Association gatherings.

For further details write to The Secretary, The English Association, The University of Leicester, University Road, Leicester, LE1 7RH.

Essays and Studies 1996

Poetry and Politics

Edited by
Kate Flint

for the English Association

D. S. BREWER

ESSAYS AND STUDIES 1996
IS VOLUME FORTY-NINE IN THE NEW SERIES
OF ESSAYS AND STUDIES COLLECTED ON BEHALF OF
THE ENGLISH ASSOCIATION
ISSN 0071-1357

© The English Association 1996

All Rights Reserved.
Unauthorised publication contravenes applicable laws

First published 1996
D. S. Brewer, Cambridge

D. S. Brewer is an imprint of Boydell & Brewer Ltd
PO Box 9, Woodbridge, Suffolk IP12 3DF, UK
and of Boydell & Brewer Inc.
PO Box 41026, Rochester, NY 14604-4126, USA

ISBN 0 85991 504 2

British Library Cataloguing in Publication Data
Poetry and politics. – (Essays and studies; v. 49)
1. English poetry – History and criticism 2. English poetry – Political aspects
I. Flint, Kate
821'.09
ISBN 0859915042

The Library of Congress has cataloged this serial publication:
Catalog card number 36-8431

This publication is printed on acid-free paper
Typeset by Rowland Phototypesetting Ltd, Bury St Edmunds, Suffolk
Printed in Great Britain by
St Edmundsbury Press Ltd, Bury St Edmunds, Suffolk

Contents

Preface	vii
THE ENGLISH REVOLUTION AND THE END OF RHETORIC: JOHN TOLAND'S *CLITO* (1700) AND THE REPUBLICAN DAEMON Nigel Smith	1
TRADE WINDS Timothy Morton	19
ISLAND QUEENS: NATIONALISM, QUEENLINESS AND WOMEN'S POETRY 1837–1861 Helen Groth	42
THE POLITICS OF A FEMINIST POETICS: 'ARMGART' AND GEORGE ELIOT'S CRITICAL RESPONSE TO *AURORA LEIGH* Louise Hudd	62
POETRY AND POLITICS IN THE 1920s John Lucas	84
PAUL MULDOON: *THE ANNALS OF CHILE* Clair Wills	111
LICENCE Robert Smith	140
Notes on Contributors	162

Preface

The American poet and essayist Adrienne Rich, in her recent volume *What is found there. Notebooks on Poetry and Politics* (1993), examines a multitude of connections between the two terms, poetry and politics. She writes forcefully, urgently of how 'poetry can break open locked chambers of possibility, restore numbed zones to feeling, recharge desire', and how these energies are crucially linked to all the conditions of our being. She violently repudiates the idea that poetry is powerless – an idea which she finds is all too prevalent in contemporary America, and which surely infects other Western societies as well – or that it is detached from the powers that organize us as a society, as communities within that society, or in particular relationships within those communities. Rather, she argues for poetry's necessity, and she does this through copious quotation from a range of writers. Some points of reference are familiar – Dickinson's troublesome volcano; Whitman's pages crammed with 'the working-man and working-woman', with 'forbidden voices/Voices of sexes and lusts'; Wallace Stevens and W.H. Auden. Many writers may well be less well known, such as Audre Lorde and Muriel Rukeyser, Gloria Anzaldúa and Minnie Bruce Pratt, June Jordan and Judy Grahn. Many of these are writing against the grain of their society, writing as African-Americans or Jewish, as lesbians, as Chicana women or Native Americans, as confirmed environmentalists: writing, in other words, from the margins, and often deliberately traversing linguistic or gender or geographical boundaries. Many of Rich's examples, too, are drawn from writers who have experienced extremes of poverty, or of war, or of brutalised discrimination, or, at the very least, who have witnessed such extremes, regarding them as inseparable from the experiences of the communities from which they come and to which they owe personal and poetic allegiance. For those whose most traumatic moments lie in the deepest pasts – as in the case of the remarkable poet Irena Klepfisz, born in 1941 in the Warsaw Ghetto, an escapee, with her mother, after the 1943 bombardment which killed her father – every act of memory becomes a political as well as a private act. Adorno's statement that 'after Auschwitz, to write a poem is barbaric' is, at the very least, called into question by Kepfisz's work, although, as

Rich quietly comments, this remark 'might be pondered by all poets who too fluently find language for what they have not yet absorbed'.

During the course of the prose pieces which make up her volume, Rich derives a number of stimulating observations about the essential connections between poetry and politics from the plethora of powerful writers upon whom she draws. To write poetry, she shows, is to refuse to remain passive. It enables one to access, through the imagination, that which has become literally unspeakable: one property of poetic language is 'to engage with states that themselves would deprive us of language and reduce us to passive sufferers.' It is to assert the possibility of creation, of recreation. The incendiary feelings which kindle poetry, and which poetry kindles, are analogous to resistance movements, underground organisations: 'Poetry, in its own way, is a carrier of the sparks, because it too comes out of silence, seeking connection with unseen others.' Moreover, in less figurative terms, poetry is important because it is portable: the workings of the imagination may easily be smuggled on a scrap of paper, a bar of soap and, of course, in the memory. A poem is more memorable than a novel or a play; it is more readily linked to oral culture with its own possibilities for transmitting history. More than anything else, 'it's imagination that must be taken hostage, or terrorized, or sterilized, in order for a totalizing unitary power to take control of people's lives', and in this light, the role of poetry in resistance, in struggle – however exotic, however quotidian the terrain of that struggle may be – is irreplaceable. Simultaneously, the political needs to partake of the same qualities that give true poetry its value: 'Politics *is* imagination or it is a treadmill – disintegrative, stifling, finally brutalizing – or ineffectual.' Imagination, feeling, honesty: the qualities that matter in politics are, for Rich, the same as those which matter in poetry. In neither sphere can one operate simply with good intentions: both must be infused with energetic conviction.

Famously – perhaps with irony, certainly with frustration – Auden wrote that 'poetry makes nothing happen; it survives/In the valley of its saying where executives/Would never want to tamper'. The world of poetry, in his elegy to Yeats, is one temporarily severed from the raw mainstream of modernity. Manifestly, his pessimism, here and elsewhere ('Poets are, by the nature of their interests and the nature of artistic fabrication, singularly ill-equipped to understand politics . . .') is misplaced. Poets may not necessarily engage with political analysis of a theoretical kind in their work, but they tap the same emotions, the same senses of injustice or anger or even elation that lie at the heart of political life. Against Auden's aloofness one might place American critic bell hooks writing of the southern black community in which she grew up. For her, encountering poetry in school, and in her working-class household – the 'one literary expression that was absolutely respected' there – 'poetry was the place for the secret voice, for all that could not be directly stated or named. Poetry was privileged speech – simple at times, but never ordinary. The magic of poetry was transformation; it was words changing shape, meaning and form. Poetry was not mere recording of the way we southern black folks talked to one another, even though our language was poetic. It was transcendent speech. It was meant to transform consciousness, to carry the mind and heart to a new dimension'.

What all the essays in this volume share is an interest in the power of poetic language to shape and to transform consciousness; sometimes in blatantly didactic ways, sometimes in more subtle, perhaps more insidious ones. The forms of politics they treat are various: ranging from the symbolic centre of Victoria's court to the angry class dissatisfaction of post First World War England; from feminist debate to the language of trade and commerce. What many of them share is an interest in nationalism, and in the question of topographical and linguistic boundaries: issues as relevant to the history of English poetry, both past and current, as to the American context of which Rich writes. The writers read poetry politically, and they take politics as the subject of their analysis; they demonstrate how poetic rhetoric cannot be severed from the wider rhetoric of public persuasion, and they interrogate, though cannot dismantle, the relationship between the two terms.

Once more, Rich provides a convenient point of entry. 'Any truly revolutionary art', she postulates, 'is an alchemy through which waste, greed, brutality, frozen indifference, "blind sorrow," and anger are transmuted into some drenching recognition of the *What if?* – the possible. *What if* – ? – the first revolutionary question, the question the dying forces don't know how to ask.' The opening essay, by Nigel Smith, directly poses the question: 'When was the first revolutionary poetry in England?': poetry that went beyond its traditional public role of praise and blame, and started to shape the imagining of the future, building on Spenser and Milton, 'the prophetic poetry of the reformed English nation', and pointing towards

Romanticism. Smith builds his argument around John Toland's *Clito* (1700). This work is not particularly remarkable for its intrinsic poetic qualities, but, combining an alertness to the contemporary political situation with an understanding of the rhetorical shifts and manoeuvres both of classical rhetoric and Miltonic epic, it is a work which transferred public oratory into poetical form in its call for liberty.

Nigel Smith demonstrates that one facet of *Clito*'s modernity lies in the way in which the force of eloquence in Toland's work derives from his views about the role of money and its circulation. Timothy Morton, in 'Trade Winds', also deals with the relationship between the tropes of trade and poetic language. He examines the importance of the spice-trade to readings of *Paradise lost*, Dryden's *Annus Mirabilis*, and Shelley's Queen Mab: it is a topos which may invoke both the attraction of the richly oriental and the dangers of luxury. At a more figurative level, Morton shows how the intertextuality entered into through the re-workings of this topos shows poetry itself to involve, like overtly commercial enterprises, both trade and plunder.

In analyzing the 'pervasive presence of the concept of queenliness in Victorian women's poetry', Helen Groth explains how this concept came to play a central part in the formation of a coherent vision of England's duty to its empire. Examining poems by Elizabeth Barrett, Christina Rossetti, Sarah Ellis and Caroline Norton, she demonstrates how women poets made Victoria the repository for a range of narratives: professional, domestic, religious and national: importantly, she shows that these poets differed widely in their perception of Victoria, 'complicating a simple dichotomous picture of women identifying with their Queen as part of a narrative of female assertiveness or domestic submission'. Gender politics are at the heart of another piece on Victorian poetry, too: Louise Hudd's analysis of George Eliot's 'Armgart' as a dialogue with Barrett Browning's *Aurora Leigh*, both in terms of its form and its content. She sees 'Armgart' as a political critique of the idealistic feminism of the verse-novel, and, in particular, takes issue with the earlier text's problematic depiction of class politics and social reform. Both poems explore the obligations of the exceptional woman to her society and to other women, 'raising the issue of what it means to be marginalised in the interests of a political action which might liberate only the exceptional few rather than the many', but, Hudd argues, Eliot had a far shrewder idea about what it meant, politically, to be involved with the necessary process of developing a socially effective feminist poetics.

Even more directly focusing on class issues, John Lucas takes as his starting point T.S. Eliot's comment of 1921 that 'the whole of contemporary politics oppresses me with a continuous physical horror'. He hypothesises that what especially troubles Eliot is the growing industrial unrest in England, and finds similar shudders at the working classes in the slouching form of Yeats's 'rough beast'. Both these poets were dedicated to 'saving civilization': against their version of what this might entail, he pits the politically radical Ivor Gurney and Edgell Rickword. Gurney's radicalism is located in his First World War experiences, and in his anger at the way in which soldiers, after the war, were 'cast off by the very nation on whose behalf they had vastly endured suffering'; Rickword he shows to be a poet concerned not just with the moribundity of post-war culture, but with finding a satisfactory form with which to combat it. He distrusted poetry which used myth as a way of foreclosing on the complexities of history – the contrast with Eliot is clear: for both, the way forward lies in democracy.

The complexities of history, of internationalism, of the postmodern world might well be said to characterise the challenging, allusive and exciting work of Paul Muldoon, whose recent collection of thematically linked poems *The Annals of Chile* (1993) forms the focus of Clair Wills's piece. In this, she shows Muldoon's fascination with the tricky business of differentiating past, present and future in the ways in which one makes sense of one's life, and links this to the interconnectedness which can be seen to take place at a more global level, 'as superficially different political cultures turn out to have many disturbing similarities'. Thus Ireland has its parallels with Chile; the eighteenth century with the twentieth. But patterns of repetition, whilst having an almost incantatory function, also contain difference, as Muldoon's incorporation of the politics of the family into his work shows: in becoming a father, in reproducing the generational cycle, he is also creating something different. And yet, as Wills points out, neatly exemplifying how interconnectedness and division are enmeshed in Muldoon's writing, 'it is unlikely that he intends to present this rather wholesome, organic metaphor without irony'.

Finally, Robert Smith engages in some essential questioning about the very nature of the presumed connection between 'poetry' and 'politics' on which the existence of this volume rests. Starting from the position that 'the poetic *can always* – even if, in the instance, it does not – annul its engagement with the 'political', and claiming that it is the essential trait of freedom which characterises the poetic, he draws on Levinas's work on ethics in order to interrogate the nature of this supposed freedom, poetic 'licence'. Through readings of Milton and Paul Celan, he engages with the topics of religion, law and memory in order to show how, in fact, poetry and politics are inescapably connected.

Theoretical reflection about the relationship between poetry and politics is a necessary activity: one that forces us to interrogate the nature of the coupling, itself rhetorically enacting, through the ready neatness of its alliteration, the apparent indissolubility of the bond. Such reflection is in itself the product of certain types of freedom: freedom within academic discourse, and beyond that, the relative freedoms endowed by material circumstances. As Rich has written elsewhere, 'every mind resides in a body'. Theory, to put it bluntly, is rarely born out of hunger or pain: poetry may well be. Poetry, Audre Lorde has reminded us, 'Is Not a Luxury'. At any rate, it *should* not be: rather, it may perform the role of a survival tool, a rebellious intervention, a means of challenging complacency of emotion or of intellect. Like politics, it draws from the past, but it also moves towards the future. Lorde writes: 'Poetry is the way we help give names to the nameless so it can be thought. The farthest horizons of our hopes and fears are cobbled by our poems, carved from the rock experiences of our daily lives . . . In the forefront of our move towards change, there is only poetry to hint at possibility made real.'

References

hooks, bell: *Talking Back. thinking feminist, thinking black* (Boston: South End Press, 1989)
Lorde, Audre: *Sister Outsider* (Freedom, CA: The Crossing Press, 1984)
Rich, Adrienne: *What is found there: Notebooks on Poetry and Politics* (1993; London: Virago, 1995)

The English Revolution and the End of Rhetoric: John Toland's Clito (1700) and the Republican Daemon

NIGEL SMITH

WHEN WAS THE FIRST revolutionary poetry in England?[1] When was the first poetry that called for radical changes in social, political and intellectual practice? In the Romantic era, there was such a verse, perhaps best known today in Blake's calls for spiritual enlightenment and in Shelley's intense and complicated visions of a socialist, sexually libertarian and vegetarian future. But how was this state of poetic awareness reached, and what has it to do with Romanticism's native resources, the prophetic poetry of the reformed English nation, in which different kinds of religious liberty were heroically treated – the poetry of Spenser and Milton?

The printed and manuscript poetry that celebrated the establishment of a republic in 1649 largely obeyed the rules of panegyric, however much it warped or inverted conventions and expectations (Smith (1994), 276–94). The spirit of a free state as against Stuart tyranny was frequently invoked but the work of programmatic suggestions for reform in church and state was left to the prose forms of advocacy and controversy. Some verse, notably Milton's and George Wither's, occupies a transitional site, in that its explores the realms of subjective inner space (that great theme of the Puritan Revolution and its literature) in terms of the religious and political achievements of the Revolution. But the participants of the Civil War and the Revolution (Milton included – for all of the creative fusing of discursive categories in his writings) thought that the words that did the work of change belonged to the category of rhetoric and oratory, not poetry.

In fact the sharpest political mind of the seventeenth-century thought that the Civil War was a direct consequence of rhetoric,

---

[1] For a recent discussion of the transformation of the word 'revolution' in the period, see Rachum.

2   THE ENGLISH REVOLUTION AND THE END OF RHETORIC:

and the following essay shows how classical rhetoric, in its starkest definition as words that have the power to effect massive transformations in human thought and action, came to be situated in poetry, over and against poetry's traditional public role of praise and blame. In taking into itself the matter of rhetoric, poetry ceased to praise or blame, or even to justify, advocate and prophesy. It began to shape the imagining of the future in the service of a kind of enlightened modernity.

When Thomas Hobbes wrote *Leviathan* using the tools of classical rhetoric (having hitherto attempted to write his science of politics logically and even geometrically), he was, it has been said, capitulating to the successful method of the 'democratical gentlemen' who were about to form a republic (Skinner, 433–36). He understood that the victory of the Parliament and the Puritans was a victory of the spoken word and the paper bullet as well as the sword, and, so Professor Skinner's argument goes, if you cannot beat them, join them. Hence, *Leviathan* is a deeply rhetorical text, despite Hobbes' previous attempt to banish rhetoric from his science of politics. The 1640s was indeed a period when the speech act found new roles for itself. By dint of his education, Hobbes thought of these innovations as examples of classical rhetoric and he tended to elide them with his identification of the king's enemies as classical republicans. In actual fact, we would also have to credit the power of persuasion to various kinds of religious language (notably prophecy) and legal rhetoric, not merely classical rhetoric. Nonetheless, the Commonwealth also thought of itself as a publicly rhetorical society, in a way that had not been the case before. This was so even during the Protectorate, when the opportunities for being openly rhetorical were more limited. What had been the possession of courtly orators (perhaps extended to the special privileges of the stage) before 1640 became the confident possession of citizens during the Interregnum (Achinstein, chs. 1, 3; Norbrook; Smith (1994), ch. 1). Some of the republicans who challenged the legitimacy of the Protectorate, some of whom conspired to assassinate Oliver Cromwell, believed strongly in a rhetorical society, in which all freemen would have an education in the political 'mysteries' of state, and the liberty to voice their views in public through the arts of eloquence (and this was conceived as involving print as well as oratory). These figures campaigned for a reborn version of classical Rome and Greece; some of them even campaigned for a new theatre of anti-tyrannical drama based on the Greek model, over and against the weakness of court-influenced drama and Davenant's proposals for a 'drama' of images and music that would indoctrinate the masses with authoritarian ideas (Smith (1995)).

For his part, Hobbes was saying that oratory was as open and as dangerous as were the weapons of war. Acts of oratory opened a chasm in the social order, and in the space between orator and audience, that threatened to disrupt order and authority. Life is art, and art is life: 'in raising passion from opinion, it is no matter whether the opinion be true or false, or the narration historical or fabulous; for, not the truth, but the image, maketh passion: and a tragedy, well acted, affecteth no less than a murder'. (Hobbes (1640), 175). In *Leviathan*, the image of the audiences' mouths chained to the mouth of the orator, usually an image of rhetorical eloquence, represents the power of the sovereign (Hobbes (1651), 263–4).

John Hall's 1652 translation of Longinus's *On the Sublime* (where sublime poetry is assumed to flourish best in a free state), describes the orator in his dedicatory epistle (to Bulstrode Whitelocke) as a kind of Hobbesian sovereign, smiting the populace with a 'cone' of words. He appears to follow Hobbes, but he was writing on behalf of the republic, and openly expressed his deep aversion to Hobbes' theories of sovereignty. In the ancient world, says Hall, orators spoke to larger audiences, while with print, only a few or one are addressed: modern politicians should be 'forming all our thoughts in a Cone, and smiting with the point' (Longinus, 188). What at first appeared to be Hobbesian is in fact a kind of democratic acknowledgement of a new audience in the arena of oratory: the reader of the pamphlet and the newsbook.

All of this was to change at the Restoration, and this was the distinct desire of the first Restoration governments (Seaward, 74). Public debate, such as had been tolerated even under the Protectorate, ended, oppositional pamphleteering became sparse, under the eye of a new censorship, and Hobbes' own writing in *Behemoth* reduced itself to a mechanistic explanation of rebellion. Direct address (except perhaps on matters of religious controversy) was replaced by oblique allegorizing, as had been the case before 1640. *Narrative* replaced oratory (that is, occurred without being classified as part of a rhetorical argument, a *narratio*) as the primary public mode, even among the sometime proponents of oratory: witness *Paradise Lost*. And if Puritan culture was to make use of the narrative trope of pilgrimage, no longer as a figure of deliverance (as it was

4 THE ENGLISH REVOLUTION AND THE END OF RHETORIC:

between 1640 and 1660), but as one of resistance amidst persecution, the picaresque mock-heroic allegorical narratives generated by Royalists during their moment of defeat in the 1650s became the dominant mode of triumph in the Restoration. Edmund Gayton's commentary on Cervantes' *Don Quixote* (1654), with its covert defence of Royalism, was superseded by Samuel Butler's openly hostile burlesque *Hudibras* (1661).

This is the view presented in Paula Backscheider's study of Restoration to Regency public exchange (Backscheider, 1–67). She shows how the restored monarchy relied heavily upon theatrical images, appropriating the anti-Puritan imagery of pre-1660 Royalist propaganda for the purpose of extending the image of monarchical authority. Note that this is an account of publicly-exchanged political meanings; not the deliberations of courtiers and aristocrats, or Whig conspirators, behind closed doors. The monstrous body of Oliver Cromwell in 1640s and 1650s play pamphlets became the figure over which the image of Charles II stood in the painted decorations for the return of the monarchy (Ogilby). Furthermore, 'opposition' only became possible within these paradigms, generated by an inherently theatrical political culture.

Some of these claims are eminently contestable. To deny a role for the arts of eloquence in the making of 'opposition' literature outside of the theatre is to miss the survival in the Restoration of the ideals and public strategies of the Commonwealth supporters, albeit in altered form (Keeble, 68–93). Yet this thesis does catch in large measure the official (and some oppositional) attitudes towards eloquence that prevailed in the Restoration. But the conditions Professor Backscheider analyses changed again after the Glorious Revolution, and in these new conditions was produced a new kind of verse that incorporated the oratorical ideals of the Commonwealth years, as well as its political sentiments. Had Hobbes lived, he might have had good reason to be scared again. For the turn of the seventeenth century produced a kind of revolutionary form, an emanation of the republicanism and freethinking of these years, attempting things not seen again until the radical poetry of the Romantic era.

Just eleven years after the Glorious Revolution was published *Clito: A Poem on the Force of Eloquence* (1700), with a long quotation from Cicero's *De Oratore* on its title-page. It then gained sufficient canonical status (or was sufficiently contentious) to be published again three years later in *Poems on Affairs of State* (1703). In the preface 'W.H.' (most probably William Hewet) wrote that the poem itself 'was handed about a good while in Manuscript', before he could obtain it. On perusal, the preface writer saw not a subversiveness in the poem, but 'something so new and singular in the management of it that highly pleas'd me'. He goes on:

> I verily believe that one or two of my acquaintance were frighted, not so much at the Contents, as at the Writer's poetical Liberty in his ranting and ALMANZOR-like strain, as if they thought he would in good earnest buckle on his Armor, or fasten Wings to his shoulders, and go about to perform in person what he would gladly leave others the honour of atchieving at his persuasion.
> (Toland (1700), sig. A2^r)

Was the poem merely read in private or was it 'performed' in the public space of the coffee house? The preface highlights the crux of the theory of oratory propounded by *Clito*: that the poem would appear, in its performance, to *do* that which it would merely persuade to do. Our attention is arrested, and this was clearly meant by the author. Moreover, the association of oratorical action with one of Dryden's stage heroes is testimony to the power of the theatre in constituting stereotypes, and a point of interest to which we shall return.

The author was John Toland (1670-1721), deist (accused atheist), republican, editor of Milton, Harrington and Ludlow.[2] The poem was written either just before or during Toland's preparation of his edition of Milton, and published just after that great undertaking (although probably not by Toland himself).[3] *Clito* is in many ways in debt to the rhetorical conception of public life: an exemplary piece of what the 'democratical gentlemen' would have had, and quite in line with Toland's own professed enthusiasm for the ideals of the 'Commonwealthsmen' of the 1650s. Also relevant is the

---

[2] The most recent account of Toland's life and works is in Champion; very extensive bibliographical details are provided in Carabelli.

[3] This has worried some commentators: see Pierre Desmaizeaux, 'Some Memoirs of the Life and Writings of Mr. John Toland', in Desmaineaux, 1. xliv-vi; Ludlow, Introduction, by A. B. Worden, 25, n. 110. But even if, as Worden suggests, *Clito* may have been 'doctored' by Toland's enemies prior to publication, it is all the more remarkable how faithful the text is to Toland's republicanism, and his literary ideals. W. H.'s preface is generally sympathetic to Toland's views, and at pains to present them as not at odds with established church or state.

6   THE ENGLISH REVOLUTION AND THE END OF RHETORIC:

context of the lapse of the Licensing Act in 1695, signalling the end of Parliamentary attempts to exert licensing controls. *Clito* is an instance of the taking of oratory onto the printed page; but mere hackery it is not, nor does it contain the verbal deliquesence of Swift's *A Tale of a Tub*, the text usually associated with the 1695 lapse.

In *Clito* 'ADEISIDAEMON' ('UNSUPERSTITIOUS') replies to the wise philosopher Clito's question: 'How far the Force of Eloquence cou'd go/To teach Mankind those Truths which they mistake' (Toland (1700), 6).[4] The poem is seventeen pages of stylistically sub-Miltonic yet rhyming heroic (and hence also sub-Drydenic) verse that attempts to embody 'freedom': 'My Phrase shall clear, short, unaffected be,/And all my Speech shall like my thoughts be free' (Ibid.), whatever the price of the bondage of rhyming. The Shelleyesque name of the poem's orator is one clue, the marriage of deism and rhetoric another: this poem, dramatizing its desire to make intentions realized, is nothing more than a revolution waiting to happen. Toland manufactures an unsuperstitious daemon, but one with an oratorical power that generates a vital enthusiasm far in excess of the deist claim of a rationally-organised universe, forms of governance and human kind. The question remains: what kind of revolution does *Clito* want?

As one commentator reminds us, the name Clito recalls 'Clio' the muse of history, while 'Clito' is similar to the Greek for 'the Key' (Daniel, 66). Hewet says in his preface that *Clito* is the intended scheme of the author/orator Toland's studies. In other words, there is good reason to believe that the poem is a blueprint for the kind of deist and republican freedom that Toland so desired. *Clito* followed on the heels not only of the editions of Milton and of Harrington, but also of Toland's most controversial work, *Christianity Not Mysterious* (1696). But this work, like nearly all Toland's prose works, tends to mask its radicalism in a variety of textual veils. *Clito*, however, is poetic oratory, and being this, is able to fly so much further.

It may well be that by Clito, Toland meant Anthony Ashley Cooper, the Third Earl of Shaftesbury, Whig and influential philsopher of moral and aesthetic benevolence. Toland and Shaftesbury were to part company, in part through Toland's attraction to the future Tory Prime Minister, Robert Harley, and because Toland's

---

[4] For Toland's later use of the figure of Adeisidaemon, see Jacob, 169–70.

own views were too extreme for Shaftesbury (Champion, 214; Klein, 16, 48, 200n.). But in the late 1690s, Toland wanted Shaftesbury's ear for his agenda: the revival of Ciceronian civic religion and republican politics within the parameters of the 1689 settlement. Toland had been involved in the publication of Shaftesbury's *An Inquiry Concerning Virtue in Two Discourses* in 1699 (of which publication its author did not approve), a revised version of which would appear in the more famous *Characteristicks* (1714), although Toland's role as a shaper of this text is now doubted. On the front page of this earlier version was a quotation from Cicero, as if Toland's *Clito* was attempting to catch the attention of a possible patron by presenting empathising signals.[5]

The *narratio* of *Clito* oscillates between calls for liberty through the power of eloquence and a narrative account of the deist view of the universe. Adeisidaemon is bursting to fill his hearer with sublime effects in a refashioned, unambiguous language of Adam:

> Then shall my fertil Brain new Terms produce,
> Or old Expressions bring again in use,
> Make all Ideas with their Signs agree,
> And sooner Things than Words shall wanting be.
> Harmonious Sounds th'attentive Ear shall please,
> While artful numbers Passions lay or raise.
> (Toland (1700), 6)

As Stephen Daniel indicates, Toland was describing the process by which the true name of things was made acceptable to the populace by the powers of unsuperstitious oratory (here regarded as capable of coining new words, or resurrecting discarded [i.e. classical] ones). Nature and culture are thus reconciled in the work of an Hermetic magus turned civic orator. In a later work, Toland similarly drew attention to the Druidic recognition of the elderly Hercules as orator and protector of learning (Toland (1751), 33–5). It is as if Toland's vision is a reborn classical republic fused with an hermetic and Baconian return to a prelapsarian knowledge of the natural world.

Reading on in *Clito*, the deist universe is 'created', in a poetic cosmology that resembles Ps. 22 and Lucretius:

---

[5] *An Inquiry Concerning Virtue in Two Discourses* (1699), with a quotation from Cicero's *De Finibus Bonorum et Malorum* on the title-page. Or is the Ciceronian detail a result of Toland's influence, an attempt to show the *Inquiry* as closely related to his own project?

and God the whole
From whence all Beings their Existence have,
And into which resolv'd they find a Grave;
How nothing's, tho all things change their Form,
As that's a fly which was but now a Worm.

(Toland (1700), 8)[6]

So quite unlike the poem of Toland's great hero, Milton, *Clito* is actually debunking the universe of *Paradise Lost*, and using the poetic energies of Lucretius' creation poem to do so. The questions forbidden by Raphael now become the focus of our attention. Toland might have valued *Paradise Lost* because it displayed 'the different Effects of Liberty and Tyranny', as Dustin Griffin has noted, but his poetry goes beyond this and beyond Milton (Griffin (1988), 7). In the space of a page (eighteen lines) possible subjects of a poem whizz by: death as mere change, eternity for all, the counting of stars; the inhabitation of planets, the birth and death of planets, planetary rotation, magnetism, wind and tidal motion, seasonal change, systems of reproduction, the sources of life, soul and mind, the creation of matter. And all these 'Shall only after me be rightly nam'd.' In this role, the narrator appears to be a 'good Satan' and God at once: 'Thus quick as Thought I unconfin'd will fly/Thro' boundless Space, and vast Eternity;/ Nature to me appears in no disguize,/Nor can one Atom scape my prying Eyes.' (Toland (1700), 10; Milton (1667), 1.177; 2.148; 4.73–5; 7.165–9. To voice the demonic and the most sacred at once is to run together the voices of both Satan and God. Since both are emanations of the narrator, Toland has effectively interiorised the narrator's role in *Paradise Lost*: he takes on and then revises Milton's own cosmological signature as poet.

Cosmology is in fact a prelude to a defence of republican liberty where oratory literally threatens to replace arms: 'O Glorious LIBERTY! for thee I'll prove/The firmest Patron that e'er Tongue did

---

[6] *Clito* contains several echoes of Dryden's translation 'Lucretius: Against the Fear of Death' (see *Clito*, 8–9, Dryden, *168*; Clito, 12, Dryden, *249*). There is a further echo of Lucretius, *De Rerum Natura*, 1.44–9 in *Clito*, 17. Toland may also have seen an MS of Dryden's *Palamon and Arcite* (publ. 1700), 3.*1042* of which is echoed in *Clito*, 17: 'Or parts the Creatures are, and God the whole'. Toland read and greatly admired Dryden despite their considerable political and religious differences. For this information, I am indebted to Dr. Paul Hammond, who also suggests that Dryden may possibly have been influenced by Toland.

move;/I'll always execute what you decree,/And be the fatal scourge of Slavery./Ambitious Tyrants, proud and useless Drones,/I'll first expose, then tumble from their thrones' (Toland (1700), 10). The connection of oratory and arms is especially relevant in a context where Toland writes against the maintenance of standing armies: 'Their warlike Troops I shall with ease disband,/And conquer those who all besides command.' Later, in an attack on priestcraft, the pope's 'Triple Crown I scornfully will spurn,/And his proud Seat to heaps of rubbish turn,/Fright all his Vassals into Dens and Caves,/Then smoak to death the sacriligeous Slaves' (Toland (1700), 14). With mere words or what? Is this a testimony merely to the power of words? And are the wholly post-Miltonic figures of compassing eternity and evacuating tyrants instances of the will to power, or an image of power itself? Toland's effectiveness as an orator is attested by the mesmeric effect he had in later years in the court of the Electress Sophia of Hanover. In *Clito*, he is aware that the clarifying power of his rhetoric can hurt those he would count as friends as much as it exposes enemies. Toland's eloquence may be without ornamentation; it is not without *ornamenta* (i.e. weapons): 'He best protects who's ablest to offend' (Toland (1700), 7). It is as if the poem is split between the persuasive but uncoercive sense of virtuous oratory theorised by Cicero, and the massive power of the Longinian orator, as so acutely realised in the Commonwealth years by John Hall (see above, 3).

In this regard, the prefatory reference to Dryden's Almanzor is telling, and opens up to us the theatrical history implicit in Toland's orator. Almanzor is a character from Dryden's *The Conquest of Granada* (1672).[7] He is a common soldier who rises to become an effective ruler. Dryden's preface apologized for this 'believable' hero – roughcast in words and deeds – for he wished to dispel accusations of idealizing within the heroic drama of the Restoration stage. Perhaps inadvertently, he went too far, alienating extreme Tory and Anglican critics, who detected a *'Poeticall Free-State... where all were Monarchs (without Subjects) and all swore Allegiance to themselves'* in the character and actions of Almanzor (Leigh, 2–3).[8] That is to say, he appears to Leigh (or Butler) as a

---

[7] For Toland's views on Dryden, see above, n. 6.
[8] Nicholas Von Maltzahn has recently argued that the author of *The Censure of the Rota* was Samuel Butler (private communication).

republican, even a Leveller, in a Hobbesian state of war. Dryden's exposure of the cruelty of tyrants was received as a justification of popular sedition, and less politically-affrighted wits travestied Almanzor in the picture of an imaginary butch warrior-stud called 'Al-man-sir' (Dryden (1978), 412–13). Almanzor was the Tamburlaine of the Restoration stage, and he rapidly became currency by which the intelligentsia discussed in a sublimated way the possibility of popular rebellion – as they saw it, a return of 1649, or worse.

Toland's orator wants words to work exactly as they do for Tamburlaine in the theatrical space of Marlowe's play: they function as actions. Words, it would seem, are 'magic' (Toland's term), and do have the power to quell: 'Those hect'ring Braves, who vaunt their Force so loud,/A Patriot's Tongue can humble with the Crowd', while 'patriot' youths take to arms to defend their rights and punish tyrannous nations. And at the end of this remarkable display of power is the assertion of a republican dream, engendered in the orator by the spirit of Brutus, and other 'men Divine', that '*All goes well when Whigs and Torys join*', that is when party division disappears, usurped power is destroyed, and a 'Commonwealth' is formed (Toland (1700), 11). For one commentator, these lines are 'frankly seditious', and a rare instance in Toland's published writings of the confession of his republicanism, which he celebrated annually by drinking with the Calves-Head Club, who met to celebrate the execution of Charles I in 1649, and which put him in touch with the more plebeian traditions of London radicalism (Evans, 63–4).[9] By 1700, Toland believed that in the common man was the real measure of intelligibility (as opposed to the elites generated by priestcraft and aristocracy). Toland's republic, like his theory of oratory, had the common man, with his common sense, at its core (Paulson (1996), 7–8).

This takes us to a typical change of gear in the poem, which should be regarded as one of its many compromises, for what follows after this poetic 'creation' of a free state is praise of William III in the context of the temporary interruption to the wars with France

---

[9] Toland was apparently expelled from Oxford in part for 'justifying the murder of Charles I'. The division usually made betwen the Calves-Head clubbers and the more literate, aristocratic or 'Roman' Whigs does not seem to me to be entirely satisfactory, and is a subject worthy of further investigation. This is especially so in the light of recent work on the clientele of the Restoration coffeehouse: see Pincus.

after the Treaty of Ryswick of 1697.[10] The poem effectively stops its own impulses and side slips into a praise of mixed monarchy, and the ideal of the 'matchless Hero' prince (a forerunner to the 'patriot King' of the Bolingbrokian opposition to Walpole's administration) (Gerard). *Clito* picks up rhetorical energy in the next section, against priestcraft, and appears to resolve the oratory/arms confusion in a truly Miltonic moment: an Areopagitican 'dinging of coits' imaged through the Vallombrosan fallen leaves in hell: 'their foolish Books (as Leaves/From Trees in Autumn fall) I'll scatter wide,/ And show those Fables which they fain wou'd hide.'[11]

The point is that the politics of 1700 are a compromise, as the politics of 1649 were not: all was at stake then. Toland can only confront politics with a series of unanswered questions. He claims a 'matchless Hero' (Toland (1700), 11) can effect the reforms that his rhetoric can only 'conceive', and the implied hero is William III. Indeed, William becomes the desired other of the orator's will: the agent who can achieve reform. But the orator appears to want to make the reforms himself. His decidedly anti-monarchical and pro-republican oratory in this context permits such reforming agency for the virtuous citizen. William is certainly praised, but Toland makes more of hailing the advantages of an elective monarchy, in order to avoid the danger of degeneration by inheritance (Toland (1700), 12), quite contrary to the arrangements by which William ruled. The praise of William still leaves the question 'where's the HERC'LES to redeem the Age?' (Toland (1700), 14), but the poet cannot name an alternative polity to that provided by the 1689 settlement.

Instead, there is a transference of energies into those areas where revolutions and renovations can take place. Toland certainly thought that politics and religion were interconnected: his good Satanic narrator frees the world (not just the nation state) by recreating the image of God:

---

[10] The period after the Treaty of Ryswick saw a considerable rise in classical republican sentiment. This is comparable to the republican speculation expressed in print after Battle of Worcester, September 1651, which effectively secured the Commonwealth from the Stuart threat.

[11] See Milton, *Areopagitica*, *CPW*, II. 562: 'When a man . . . hath furnisht out his findings in all their equipage, drawn forth his reasons as it were a battell raung'd, scatter'd and defeated all objections in his way'; idem., *Paradise Lost*, 1.301–3: 'who lay entranced/Thick as autumnal leaves that strew the brooks/ In Vallombrosa.'

12 THE ENGLISH REVOLUTION AND THE END OF RHETORIC:

> When I've perform'd these Feats, new Danger calls;
> From Earth I'll soar, and scale high Heaven's Walls
> To pull false Gods from thence, that Men may see
> There's but one, true, all-perfect DEITY. (Toland (1700), 16)

And Hell itself is abolished by a recounting of its traditional literary images which are then denied: an iconoclastic act that echoes the latter sections of *Paradise Regained*. Yet here Satan is not despatched below, to fight another day, but abolished, just as his Miltonic energies have been assumed (a hundred years ahead of Blake) by the revolutionary narrator: 'Legions of Fiends to Atoms I'll reduce,/ And leave bad Men no Temter for excuse.' Toland out-Miltons Milton as he remakes God, abolishes Satan, reconstructs the orator, and interiorizes religion not as Puritan prophecy but as republican civic religion. This was a remarkable feat, for John Dennis described Milton as the 'most daring Genius that has appear'd in the World' (Dennis (1701), 333). Implicitly, Toland exposes what he regarded as the sacerdotal residue in Milton. Another section argues similarly for the immortality of the soul. It is here that the dream of rhetoric finds its fulfilment: 'So shall my Words like Thunderbolts be hurl'd,/And will confound or mend the erring World.' (Toland (1700), 20)

Still another important context for the 1690s is relevant, as the force of eloquence in Toland's work is to be rooted in his views on the role of money. In the context of the founding of the Bank of England, the concern with paper money, and the debate on public finance in the 1690s, Toland published in 1696 (four years after Locke's first treatise on money) a translation of the sixteenth-century Italian thinker, Bernardo Davanzati's *A Discourse upon Coins*. Davanzati's aristotelian lecture of 1588 is unremarkable and conservative for its views (it does not understand the principles of paper money) except when we relocate it within Toland's pantheism and deism. In terms of the cosmology set out in *Clito*, Davanzati's description of money is understandable as a natural force (gold and silver living bodies, alchemically distilled by the sun and internal heat in the bowels of the earth) that circulates as the 'second blood' and 'living member' of a state.[12]

---

[12] Later elaborated in Toland (1751 [Eng. trans.]), 28–33, where rocks and metals are described as alive (the former as the earth's teeth) until they are extracted.

What is an analogy in Davanzati becomes quite literal within Toland's system:

> Hence it may be easily conceiv'd that every *State* must have a quantity of *Blood* to circulate therein. But as the *Blood* stopping on the Head or the larger Vessels puts the *Body* naturally into a Consumption, Dropsy, or Apoplexy, *&c.* so should all the *Money* be only in a few Hands, as in those of the rich for Example, the *State* falls unavoidably into Convulsions, and other dangerous Distempers. (Toland (1751), 18)

It is not merely that the lowering of interest rates raises the value of money (as recommended by Locke), but that the circulation of these vital bodies, from rich purses into poor, and back again, guarantees the continuity and strength of the state. In fact, money is the force of circulation that replaces in Toland's system the reciprocity of the economic and rhetorical systems of the Renaissance (Hutson, 52–85). It is imagined in this way precisely because it is categorised within Toland's vitalistic materialism. *Eloquentia* redefined as the revolutionary force of *Clito* is the means for the populace (identified as the orator's audience), to see this truth. Davanzati's reference to the valuing of money in Roman temples is attractive to Toland because it is a vision of the role of money in the civic religion that he imagines will emerge shortly in the deist future. It is, of course, a literalisation within the new civic religion of the metaphor of grace as money in Christian theology. After the sermon of eloquence comes the sacrament of public valuation in the Temple of Juno (Toland (1700), 25–6), an exquisitely republican and Harringtonian perception. At this time, Toland had access to (and would eventually translate) works by the hermetic philosopher Giordano Bruno (Daniel, 203–4). Brunian and Hermetic cosmology and geology provide an animated system that fuses natural and social circulation.

The response to Toland's poem, in printed form at least, reinserted him into the world of party politics and petty controversy. S.F.'s *Mr Toland's Clito examined*, written in October 1700, but not published until 1702, assumes that Toland wrote his own preface in an attempt at self-publicity. One major element in its attack is to suggest that Toland is sexually licentious, and that his poetry is but a thin disguise for his libido. The address towards the end of *Clito* to the female figure of Victorina might lead one to concur with S.F.:

14 THE ENGLISH REVOLUTION AND THE END OF RHETORIC:

> BUT, when from Care and public Business free,
> Bright VICTORINA my lov'd Theme shall be,
> The softest Words the sweetest Things will tell,
> And all I write or speak be fine and well.
> When she inspires, I must great pursue;
> If she approv'd, what wonders cou'd I do?
> (Toland (1700), 20–1)

To the modern ear, it seems almost self-parodic in tone, and the preface conspires with this effect (Sullivan, 189).[13] And yet it could equally be argued that Toland was describing heterosexual love as the 'token of a final trancendence which would transform the sage's confrontation with the universe into participation' (See Champion, 196, 205n., 222n., 230–1). Toland was later to replace Christ on the cross with the female figure of Nature, an acknowledgement, it has been argued, that all forms of contemplation involved desire on the art of the perceiver, as opposed to Shaftesbury's notions of disinterested aesthetic inquiry (Paulson (1996), 29, 43).

The poem is, in S.F.'s view, an atheistical 'Rant indeed'. The figure of the orator is reversed in an anti-republican description of an 'ochlocracy': 'He may move His Tongue long enough before his *Prosaic Poetry* can lead us into the mistake of making chains for our selves, and seeking imaginary Good before that which is real.' Where Toland tries to hide his republicanism (or does he?) in the structure of his poem, S.F. finds him out unproblematically. There is a resistance to writing on Toland's terms, but finally a capitulation in a bawdy, negative sublime: 'Now our Spark's for *soaring*, when, though he is not so swag Belly'd as father *Dommimick*, yet his Guts, like his, were never made for *Mounting*.' (Toland (1700), 8).

Toland's poetry is further explained by a consideration of the works of his associate, the critic and playwright John Dennis. Dennis is remembered as a Whig sympathiser and an objector to priestcraft, like Toland, although not a deist (he disavowed it in print). But Pope's attacks on Dennis in the *Essay on Criticism* are not merely because Pope's preference for French neoclassical order found Dennis's interest in effects of terror and the sublime repulsive.

[13] 'Whether Victorina be only a Fiction, or the designation of a real Mistress, good manners will not let us too curiously enquire: but be this as it will, such a Character was absolutely necessary to assuage that Divinity, which (as the Poets speak) inspir'd him with so much fury befor.' (Toland (1700), iv).

Dennis's aesthetics are closely linked to his republicanism (however much – again like Toland – he hid this in panegyric for William III) (Dennis (1701), 1.210, 226–7, 243, 244, 330). Thus, his essays on poetry are constructed around a 'republican' canon of texts: Lucan (Cato's famous republican speech), Machiavelli (cited against the High Church), Milton, Harrington; some of the same classical texts as Toland (e.g. Horace, *Odes*, 3.3) (Ibid., 199). He also thought that the power of modern poetry was superior to the classics. Among the moderns, he meant not only Milton, but also the Scottish Protestant George Buchanan, whose Latin translations of the Psalms he believed superior to Virgil, because closer to the spirit of Hebrew. It is true that he knew and to a large extent followed Dryden and neoclassical aesthetic principles, but his interest in effect takes us far beyond the writing of rules: 'Passion is the principal thing in Poetry' (Ibid., 201). For Dennis, Shakespeare's genius lay in his presentation of the Roman spirit in the figures of Cassius and Coriolanus, both republican heroes. By comparison, love on the stage is a subordinate quality.

Is this not to begin to engage in precisely the same concerns and predicaments as Toland? Dennis is interested in what happens when one reads or sees as part of the audience. He has an inherently rhetorical and oratorical conception of the literary work(-even if he talks 'enthusiasm' into boringness; his poetry is sometimes genuinely 'sublime'). His *The Usefulness of the Stage* (1698) has more to do with a republican conception of anti-tyrannical drama than anything else. Dennis's example reverses Backscheider's rule: his theatricality is a consequence of, rather than a reaction against, literary republicanism. Not so either Dryden or Pope. Furthermore, Dennis claimed that he wrote in favour of a 'public spirit' (a Harringtonian phrase) that would be reprojected on the stage, just as some of the 1650s republicans (but not usually Puritans) had hoped:

> A Poet is capacitated by that which is commonly call'd Regularity, to excite the ordinary Passions more powerfully by the Constitution of the Fable, and the Influence which that must necessarily have, both upon the Words and Thoughts; and Religion, besides the Influence it will have upon the ordinary Passions, will be to a Poet, who has Force and Skill enough to make his Advantage of it, a perpetual Source of extraordinary Passions, which is commonly call'd Enthusiasm, for the sentiments and the Expressions. (Ibid., 217)

The energy of persuasion and the force of eloquence in Toland become 'extraordinary Passion', that is, 'Enthusiasm' in Dennis. But the theory of enthusiasm backs away from the confrontation that Toland wants. In Dennis, as it will be in Shaftesbury, enthusiasm is regulated.

Dennis's model of effects relies upon a deist and republican description of the world (despite his disavowal of the former position). Like Harrington, Toland's other genius, there is a mechanistic (neo-Hobbesian) account of physical objects, coupled with principles of vital animation and a universe in flux: 'Man owes... its Health... to... its boasted Reason, and the piercing Force of those aspiring Thoughts, which are able to pass the Bounds that circumscribe the Universe.' The addition of rules (bowing his head in the direction of French neoclassicism in addition to the natural power of English 'gothic' genius), is parallel to the Machiavellian and Harringtonian addition of the constitutional arts of rotation and representation to the gifts of nature and fortune. Dennis is sometimes looked upon as a law-giver, but his sense of artistic effect and the power of enthusiasm contains a vitalism that fits with the structure and intentions of Toland's poem. Yet without reason, poetical enthusiasm would run off into 'madness': the state and aesthetic perception are precariously balanced (Ibid., 233). The search for a revived 'publick spirit' is the same as the search for true religion in poetry. In the case of the latter, the search for the merging of poetry and religion is a search for what is lost: this is found in the realisation of the sublime as cause and effect of enthusiasm. Dennis's elegy on Queen Mary is an example of poetic enthusiasm, not an inconsiderable achievement by the standards of the 1690s, but still 'tamed' despite being freely pindaric (Dennis (1695)). So here, Dennis is quite unlike Toland in *Clito*. But just as Dennis's enthusiasm was a kind of selling out, and Toland's verse was forced to compromise, so, as Dustin Griffin tells us, was Milton 'assimilated' by 'acccomodation' in the eighteenth century to less incendiary tastes (Griffin, 97).

And yet this trajectory does not quite convince in the instance of *Clito*. In 1939, one of the few commentators on *Clito* claimed that the poem was to Toland as *Queen Mab* was to Shelley (Fairchild, 191–2). Ianthe in *Queen Mab* is equivalent to Toland's spirit of eloquence (Shelley, II.67–82; V.121, and c.140ff). More recently, Jon Mee has argued that some of the sources of Blake's mythography are to be found in Toland's writings on the Druids, the Egyptians and rational monotheism (Mee, 94–5, 121, 127, 137–8, 196). But where Toland praises commerce, Shelley of course does not. Toland simultaneously praises enlightenment and a monied society; by the time Blake and Shelley wrote, there was still a superstitious Church of England, but also an industrial proletariat.

Clito has been almost entirely neglected in the canon of literary criticism, and it has attracted scarcely more attention from intellectual historians. A great work it is not, but it is in fact a remarkable watershed in the transformation of poetic functions in modern history.

References

Unless otherwise stated, the place of publication is London.

Achinstein, Sharon, *Milton and the Revolutionary Reader* (Princeton, 1994).
Backscheider, Paula R., *Spectacular Politics: Theatrical Power and Mass Culture in Early Modern England* (Baltimore and London, 1993).
Butler, Samuel, *Hudibras* (1661).
Carabelli, G., *Tolandiana* (Florence, 1975).
Champion, Justin, *The Pillars of Priestcraft Shaken: The Church of England and its Enemies, 1660–1730* (Cambridge, 1992).
Cooper, Anthony Ashley, Third Earl of Shaftesbury, *An Inquiry Concerning Virtue in Two Discourses* (1699).
Daniel, Stephen H., *John Toland: His Methods, Manners, and Mind* (Kingston and Montreal, 1984).
Dennis, John, *The Advancement and Reformation of Poetry* (1701), in John Dennis, *The Critical Works*, ed. Edward Niles Hooker, 2 vols. (Baltimore, 1939).
———, *The Court of Death. A Pindarique Poem, Dedicated to the Memory of Her Most Sacred Majesty, Queen Mary* (1695).
Desmaizeaux, Pierre, 'Some Memoirs of the Life and Writings of Mr. John Toland', in Pierre Desmaizeaux, ed., *A Collection of Several Pieces of Mr. John Toland*, 2 vols. (1726), i.xliv–vi.
Dryden, John, *Works*, ed. H.T. Swedenburg, et al., vol. XI (California, 1978).
———, trans. *Palamon and Arcite* (1691).
Evans, Robert Rees, *Pantheisticon. The Career of John Toland* (New York and Bern, 1991).
F., S., *Mr Toland's Clito examined* (1702).
Gayton, Edmund, *Pleasant Notes upon Don Quixot* (1654).
Gerrard, Christine, *The Patriot Opposition to Walpole: Politics, Poetry and National Myth, 1725–1742* (Oxford, 1994).
Griffin, Dustin, *Regaining Paradise: Milton and the Eighteenth Century* (Cambridge, 1988).

18   THE ENGLISH REVOLUTION AND THE END OF RHETORIC:

Hobbes, Thomas, *The English Works*, ed. Sir William Molesworth (1840).
——, *Leviathan* (1651), ed. C. B. Macpherson (1968).
Hutson, Lorna, *The Usurer's Daughter: Male Friendship and Fictions of Women in Sixteenth-Century England* (1994).
Jacob, Margaret C., *The Radical Enlightenment: Pantheists, Freemasons and Republicans* (1981).
Keeble, N.H., *The Literary Culture of Nonconformity in Later Seventeenth-Century England* (Leicester, 1987).
Klein, Lawrence E., *Shaftesbury and the Culture of Politeness: Moral Discourse and Cultural Politics in Early Eighteenth-Century England* (Cambridge, 1994).
Leigh, Richard [?Samuel Butler], *The Censure of the Rota* (1673).
Longinus, Dionysius, *On the Sublime*, trans. John Hall (1652).
Lucretius [T. Lucretius Carus], *De Rerum Natura*.
Mee, John, *Dangerous Enthusiasm: William Blake and the Culture of Radicalism in the 1790s* (Oxford, 1992).
Ludlow, Edmund, *A Voyce from the Watch Tower, Part Five: 1660–1662*, ed. A. B. Worden (1978).
Milton, John, *Areopagitica* (1644), in *Complete Prose Works*, ed. Don M. Wolfe, et al.. 8 vols. (New Haven, 1953–84), vol. 2.
——, *Paradise Lost* (1667; 2nd edition 1674).
Norbrook, David, 'Milton's *Areopagitica*, Censorship and the Early Modern Public Sphere', in Richard Burt ed., *The Administration of Aesthetics Censorship, Political Criticism, and the Public Sphere* (Minneapolis, 1994), 3–33.
Ogilby, Sir John, *The Entertainment of His Most Excellent Majestie Charles II* (1662).
Paulson, Ronald, *The Beautiful, Novel, and Strange: Aesthetics and Heterodoxy* (Baltimore, 1996).
Steve Pincus, '"Coffee Politicians Does Create": Coffeehouses and Restoration Political Culture', *JMH*, 67 (1995), 807–34.
Rachum, Ilan, 'The Meaning of "Revolution" in the English Revolution', *JHI*, 56 (1995), 195–215.
Seaward, Paul, *The Cavalier Parliament and the Reconstruction of the Old Regime, 1661–1667* (Cambridge, 1989).
Shelley, Percy Bysshe, *Queen Mab* (1812).
Skinner, Quentin, *Reason and Rhetoric in the Philosophy of Thomas Hobbes* (Cambridge, 1996).
Smith, Nigel, *Literature and Revolution in England, 1640–1660* (New Haven and London, 1994), 276–94.
——, 'Milton and Popular Republicanism in the 1650s', in D. Armitage, A. Himy, and Q. Skinner, edd., *Milton and Republicanism* (Cambridge, 1995), 137–55.
Sullivan, Robert E., *John Toland and the Deist Controversy: A Study in Applications* (Cambridge, Mass., 1982).
Toland, John, *Christianity Not Mysterious* (1696).
——, *Clito: A Poem on the Force of Eloquence* (1700).
——, *Pantheisticon* (1720; 1751, Eng. trans.).

Trade Winds
TIMOTHY MORTON

Introduction

THE REPRESENTATION OF the trade and consumption of luxury goods played a special topical role in relationships between poetry and political conceptions of the trading status of Britain. Moreover, capitalist rhetoric was generally consistent as a template for locally diverse representations of consumption. The 'trade winds' topos, for example, was a commonplace in seventeenth, eighteenth-, and early nineteenth-century panegyrics to trade, didactic poetry and epic, employed in such works as Blackmore's *Creation* (1712), Thomson's *The Seasons* (1726–1730) and Darwin's *The Botanic Garden* (1789, 1791). The topos represented the perfumed winds, scented with spice, flowing from the islands associated with the spice trade, such as the Moluccas, towards the imaginary nose of the reader. It did not necessarily imply the actual trade winds, but they were often the literal referent of the topos. The topos was part of the contested figuration of transnational trade, the language of praise and blame. While it was employed in poems which advertise or criticize Britannia's trading powers, it was also used in the poetry of natural science, religious mystery and theodicy, and there may be many other uses of the topos besides these. The politics of the topos' figurative structures was significantly orientalist, exoticizing the lands from which the spices flow and the flows of trade themselves, and spicing up the poetry in which it was placed. Moreover, as a topos about trade, to use it was to be preoccupied with translation, or metaphor, or tropology. Consequently, it is difficult to separate its political and poetic functions.

Milton's representation of Satan through the trade winds topos in *Paradise Lost* (1667) provides ways of showing the ambiguous political significance of spice which continued for a century and a half. My discussion of Milton is followed by an analysis of Dryden's *Annus Mirabilis* (1667), and a close reading of a short extract from Shelley's early radical poem *Queen Mab* (1813). I have also included some remarks about the difficulty of making cultural-historical distinctions between spices and other foods, using Italian poetic representations of chocolate in the eighteenth century as a guide. The final section draws some conclusions about relationships between poetry and politics which arise in the discourses of the spice trade.

Milton's pharmacy

'"If God allowed the inhabitants of Paradise to trade, they would deal in fabrics and spices,"' declared Mohammed (Braudel, II, 559). Long-distance trade, including the spice trade, practised by an upper echelon of merchants, was a powerful motor of early capitalism. Historians like Jacques Heers and Peter Matthias, according to Fernand Braudel, often 'tend to place large-scale production or trade in the foreground' (Braudel, I, 382; see II, 403–408). The apparently superficial luxuries of life, however, often marketed as what Kopytoff would call 'enclaved commodities', circulated only among social elites, are not so easily distinguishable, for Braudel, from those necessities which seem to underpin 'everyday life' (see Arjun Appadurai, ed., 22). For 'What historians have called the hunger for gold, the hunger to conquer the world or the hunger for spices was accompanied in the technological sphere by a constant search for new inventions and utilitarian applications' (Braudel, I, 415). Developments in cartography beyond portulan charts, for example, involved new technologies of perspective in order to allow the Portuguese to navigate beyond the equator, around the coast of Africa and towards the spice islands in the Indian Ocean. Moreover, long-distance trade helped to create early versions of firms, and mediated between local and global trading concerns, and between pre-capitalist and capitalist economies (Braudel, I, 440; see II, 436–7).

As a granular commodity, which could be stored and transported with great ease, spice approached the status of specie. Yet it was often used as a form of payment in kind (Braudel, II, 203). *Baratto* or barter was central 'even to the Levant trade: where since before the fifteenth century, the secret of success lay in obtaining spices, pepper or gall nuts in exchange for fabrics or glass ornaments from Venice, thus avoiding paying cash' (Braudel, I, 470). Unlike the British East India Company, the Dutch East India Company used spice as an indirect mode of payment (Braudel, III, 220). The spice trade, then, always involved something tropological, aside from its figuration in poetic language. The flow of spices, their troping from east to west, substituted for gold and silver, which flowed east to saturate India and China, so that Europe's balance remained in deficit in this area, 'until as late as the 1820s' (Braudel I, 462; see II, 208). Spice gradually and sporadically assumed many roles, between food, capital and money. These roles took it beyond its status as an object of luxury consumption and its use in feast-and-fast economies, for example festivals like Christmas and Easter. Spice itself was not necessarily destined for a particular dinner plate: it was often imported in order to be recirculated, at a greater profit, in an act which the economic writer Thomas Mun (1571–1641) described as *Transitio* (Mun in Purchas, 746).

The tropological uncertainty of the spatio-temporal processes of stock markets affects Braudel's uncertainties about the nature of tropical trade. It is difficult to tell whether *le commerce d'Inde en Inde* or *inlandse handel*, to use the Dutch term, resembled a 'village market' or an 'outdoor Stock Exchange' powered by the cycling flows of the monsoon (Braudel, II, 120). Besides, long-distance European trade provided ways of synchronizing other kinds of trade, for example the spice trading-fairs of Cairo and Alexandria, which could be intercepted with a working knowledge of the movements of caravans and pilgrims (Braudel, II, 128; c.f. III, 76). The flow of commodities involved sequences of tropological substitution. Coins and glass beads left Venice for Alexandria, to be exchanged for 'pepper, spices, and drugs' and brought back to Venice to be sold at the Fondaco dei Tedeschi (Braudel, II, 140ff). On the coast of Coromandel, where the Dutch East India Company bought fabrics, the 'exchange currency was spice from the Moluccas or Japanese copper' (Braudel, II, 142). The longer the return journey, the higher the profit, even in antiquity (Braudel, II, 168). Certain goods have their luxury status thrust upon them through transportation. The Javanese, living in the spice islands themselves, were observed by Johann Albrecht Mandelslo to be inflating the price of imported *rice* in 1639 (Braudel, II, 406). There was no inherent distinction between luxury and necessity considered from the standpoint of exchange value.

Just as long-distance trade itself contained a tropological element, so too did the literary topoi which advertised, evoked and criticized it in figurative language. For example, depending on the mood of the passage concerned, spice could be imagined as the product of a fantasy land, or the specious frippery of dreams: 'worlds of abundance and of happiness, and above all of immortality, inhabited by multiple-centenarians, evergreen trees and the ineffable phoenix; and it is there that spices grow' (Montanari, 63).

The range of moods associated with the literary representation of spice is nowhere more powerfully demonstrated than in a close reading of Milton's representation of long-distance trade. Milton is significant for any study of the politics of poetic language about trade, precisely insofar as there is no firm and single political reference in his use of the trade winds topos. Milton is a good example of the autonomy of figurative language relative to its political referents. Milton's representation of the spice trade plays deviously between a topical and a tropological moment. He oscillates between conceiving of spice as a marker of the blessed space of Paradise, and spice as an unstable signifier in a chain of tropological, and mercantile, substitution. The presence of spice on both sides of the equation demonstrates the extent to which long-distance trade had permeated seventeenth-century poetics.

Spice in Milton retains the multiplicity of meanings which it had accrued in other practices and discourses. Boundaries between medicine and food, and between confectionery and nutrition within the category of food, were not fixed as Europe moved towards capitalism. And narratives about the value of substances traded over transnational distances were associated with orientalist legends of medicinal riches. Networks of trade established modes of evaluation. Nicolás Monardes' popular herbal on medicinal products from the West Indies (1569) was translated from Spanish into English as *Ioyfull Newes out of the New-found Worlde* (1596). Along with a dialogue on the virtues of iron and a little treatise on the medicinal properties of snow, it contains a treatise on the 'Bezar' (bezoar) stone, removed from a giant hart, and the herb 'Escuerconera', mythical medicines like unicorn's horns. The Portuguese pay high prices to the Indians for these stones, 'that they doo so take out, and they carrye them to the *China*, to sell: and from thence to *Maluco*, and from *Maluco* to *Calicut*, for there is the greatest utterance of them, and they do esteeme so much of them, that one is woorth there, beeing fine, fiftie crownes as they are here' (Monardes, fol. 122).

Value is bound up with translation, tropological substitution and trade. From the very beginning of Milton's poem, God is described as being worshipped with 'Ambrosial odours and ambrosial flowers' (II.246). 'Odours' may imply spices burnt in sacrifice. Satan, however, is the exemplar of the tropical use of spice. He is associated with threatening processes of trade, translation, intoxication and metaphor. He traps Eve like Hamlet trapping his uncle, 'Tropically' (III.ii.216). This indicates a larger problematic in Milton's figurative register. Milton's use of epic simile in the context of theodicy suggests that trade and processes of intoxicating fancy have always existed in the garden of Paradise. Topos is grounded in tropos. Place, indeed the ultimate place of places, exists within a broader context of space and spacing, crossing spaces and reaching other shores, moving towards or away from spaces. Eve can dream and Adam can be carried away on linguistic flights of fancy. Spices can be enjoyed and the first humans can luxuriate in the sensual. The poetics of prehistory is being mediated through the long historical narratives and discourses of trade.

Descriptions of the devils in the opening books of *Paradise Lost* are often orientalist, but Milton does not let the occident off the hook. The orient is the place of meeting between European and Asian traders. It is the place of luxury trade. The devils are described as being like merchants flocking to 'Ormus' (II.2–4): Ormuz, in the Persian Gulf, was an important site for the jewel trade. In book II, Satan is described as a trader leaving the Moluccas or spice islands, and hugging their shores with his ship as he sails southwest towards the Cape of Good Hope. Here Milton uses the trade winds topos:

> As when far off at sea a fleet descried
> Hangs in the clouds, by equinoctial winds
> Close sailing from Bengala, or the isles
> Of Ternate and Tidore, whence merchants bring
> Their spicy drugs: they on the trading flood
> Through the wide Ethiopian to the Cape
> Ply stemming nightly toward the pole. (II.636–42)

'The trading flood' may be explained as the place where the trade winds blow. 'Bengala' is modern Bengal, while Ternate and Tidore are islands in the Moluccas. The 'spicy drugs' anticipate the apple. The image also anticipates the moment at which Satan approaches Eden. In a wonderful demonstration of narrative continuity, book IV describes him as a trader excited to be approaching the exotic scents of the coast of Mozambique and the island of Madagascar, mediated through archaic topoi about *Arabia felix*. The trade winds topos sounds again:

> and of pure now purer air
> Meets his approach, and to the heart inspires

> Vernal delight and joy, able to drive
> All sadness but despair: now gentle gales
> Fanning their odoriferous wings dispense
> Native perfumes, and whisper whence they stole
> Those balmy spoils. As when to them who sail
> Beyond the Cape of Hope, and now are past
> Mozambic, off at sea north-east winds blow
> Sabean odours from the spicy shore
> Of Arabie the blest, with such delay
> Well pleased they slack their course, and many a league
> Cheered with the grateful smell old Ocean smiles.
> So entertained those odorous sweets the fiend
> Who came their bane.   (IV.153–67)

(There is a similar passage in Diodorus Siculus' account of *Arabia felix*; Diodorus Siculus, 85.) Thus, while seemingly closer to Eden, Satan as the merchant has now doubled back on his course and is travelling in a northeasterly direction around the Cape of Good Hope. Is Satan approaching or leaving a place here? There is a remarkable ambiguity of movement, forwards to Eden or backwards within the similes. A distance is established between figurative language and what it represents. Milton, whose very syntax sustains the warp and weft of his ideas, cannot have meant this by accident. As the poetic location of likeness, simile should lead the reader towards a contemplation of the harmonious relationships between what is described and the process of description. Here, figurative language is a kind of trafficking in meaning which may not embody reality, but only remain contiguous with it.

The Portuguese had mastered the particular trade route around the coast of Africa to the Moluccas which the epic similes delineate. This might suggest a nationalistic impulse behind Milton's choice of imagery as a contribution to the English 'spice race', as John Keay calls it. The rise of Portugal in the wake of Vasco da Gama had 'culminated spectacularly in the direct shipment of pepper and spices to Lisbon, a revolution in itself' (Braudel, III, 139). Mozambique in particular was a Portuguese province. Madagascar was perceived as strategically important for England in the 1630s, and was invested with all manner of fantastic, utopian significance (Gilman). Luis de Camões (1524/5–1580) had written a Portuguese epic about Vasco da Gama entitled *The Lusiads* (1572), which had been translated into English by Sir Richard Fanshawe (1665), an ambassador in the Court of Spain who died in Madrid in 1666. Mozambique is described suggestively in terms of flow, evoking the circulation of trade and the ocean's currents:

> The *warlike People* the sale *Ocean* plough
> Leaving the *South*, and face the *Orient*,
> 'Twixt MADAGASCAR's Isle, where all things flow,
> And ETHIOPIA's barren Continent. (I.42)

The images of the flow of goods from a wondrous island resembles Milton's representation of the East Indies, and though it is possible to read Camões' poem as a more straightforward, less interiorized narrative than Milton's, both are about ennoblement and cupidity, and both attempted to out-trope Classical epic (see Helgerson, 155–63). Some 'specific allusions' to *The Lusiads* have been found in *Paradise Lost*, and Satan's journey has been compared with the Portuguese epic (Smith, 227). Yet, the parallels between Satan and Camões' new Argonauts, as he calls them, are not clear-cut. In terms of the rhetoric of the spice trade, Satan is acting more like the Dutch in some envious representation by a contemporary economic writer, usurping the wondrous islands, possessing nothing of value himself but only recirculating others' goods, a master of substitution.

It is also possible, however, to show that the referential instability of the similes is saying something about the tropological nature of spice, and about Satan as a figure who is himself an embodied trope, a twisting, turning character well suited to the body of a snake. In a similar fashion, Dalila is imagined in *Samson Agonistes* (1647–53?) as a merchant ship, 'an amber scent of odorous perfume / Her harbinger' (720–21). Dalila is revision of Desdemona, who is described both as a precious cargo and as the vessel in which she travels. The Moors at Mombassa in *The Lusiads* play a similar role, dissimulating about the riches to which they have access in order to gain control over Vasco da Gama's fleet:

> Moreover, if thou seek for *Merchandize*
> Produc't by the Auriferous LEVANT;
> *Cloves, Cinnamon*, and other burning *Spyce*;
> Or any good or salutiferous *Plant*;
> Or, if thou seek bright *Stones* of endless price,
> The flaming *Ruby*, and hard *Adamant*:
>   Hence thou may'st *All* in such abundance beare,
> That thou may'st bound thy *wish* and *Voyage* Here. (II.4)

Satan's voyage through sheer space, his bridging of Chaos, is described as a figuratively unstable process: is he swimming, sinking, wading, creeping or flying (II.949–50)? In contrast, the animals who walk, swim or fly in the description of creation are precisely differentiated (VII.501–504). Creation provides Chaos with a syntax by cutting into it with the word 'Silence', spoken by the Son as its inaugurating word. But the syntactical instability of Satan's journey may also be read as being about the radical, or structural, instability of the space of trade, capital and colonialism. Just as Chaos is neither empty nor full, but has a kind of spectral, ectoplasmic existence, so trade involves a processural sense of spatiotemporality which only agglutinates into something as solid as a *place* for particular, strategic reasons, which may then be abandoned in favour of another location. If trade was cutting up and re-articulating the world of the seventeenth century, it was doing so in ways that were not always as predictable and providential as the Son's verbal swordplay. The terrestrial space of trade and the extraterrestrial one of Chaos, are not so much Judaeo-Christian spatiotemporal constructs as Lucretian ones, seemingly endless fluxes of material in which a single turn, trope or *clinamen* can result in the creation of a universe.

In contrast to the uncertainty of capitalism and Chaos, the Edenic representation of spice is intended to be a topos about the correct application of tropes. Temperance in eating is the syntax of health and goodness, cutting through and articulating the sensual and material, which are then seen not as epiphenomenal to true experience, but as its divine clothing or *integumentum*. This is why Michael's vision of the lazar-house, which haunted Shelley when writing his vegetarian prose and poetry, is about the consequences of intemperate diet, and why this passage leads directly to a condemnation of the idolatry of icons (XI.466–524). To be attracted to what is on one's plate *qua* sheer sensuality, pure appearance, is to be unable to ascend the Neoplatonic ladder. In *Paradise Regained* (1667–70), Christ resists the spicy temptation of Satan's superbly-prepared meal, with its ambergris flavouring: 'Thy pompous delicacies I contemn, / And count thy specious gifts no gifts but guiles' (II.390–91). Milton is playing on the significance of 'specious', which is etymologically linked to 'spice' and 'specie', as well as to 'species', from the Latin *species*, signifying appearance and a certain lack of a universal, generic attribute. In both epics, the language of standing implies the steadfastness of individual conscience and faith, and a resistance to the tropical, twisting qualities of language which undermine the place on which one stands. But this does not mean negating the role of spice, balms and drugs, or their eroticism. In reward for his steadfastness, Jesus is rewarded with celestial food at the end of *Paradise Regained* (IV.588–90). Dalila's tomb will be visited with 'odours' or burnt spices (*Samson Agonistes*, 987). The Attendant Spirit in *Comus* (1634) leaves for the Hesperides, where 'west winds, with musky wing / About the cedarn alleys fling / Nard, and cassia's balmy smells' (988–90). Nard, found in Milton's Eden, was used to anoint Jesus' head in Mark xiv.3, 8. Indeed, it is Satan who comes as 'the bane' of the spicy 'odorous sweets' of Eden (IV.166–67). He will put an end to sensuality by peddling it.

Shelley and spice

In the literature of the following century, the rhetoric of spice played between topography and tropology, between the uneasy instability of scent, desire, flavour and drug and the fixed location of righteous consumption, love and medicine, and between the boundaries of national place and the locus of a meal, and the unstable fluctuations of commerce. The trade winds topos was deployed from different political positions throughout the seventeenth and eighteenth centuries. Milton, as we have seen, used it to suggest the mercenary quality of Satan's journey, and to establish a register of figurative instability in which spice could either be a poison or a cure. Dryden, in seeking to encourage the expansion of the British monopoly in the East Indies, poetically redirected the flow of commodities away from Amsterdam and towards London. Blackmore employed the topos to justify Britain's place at the centre of the theatre of the globe; trade was figured as the performance of divine providence. Thomson revised Dryden, justifying a later phase of colonial expansion through a paternalism which claimed that the Edenic medicines of the tropics were being wasted without profit. The botanist Erasmus Darwin (1731–1802) modified the medical mode of the topos in a panegyric to the British appropriation of a naturalized, global pharmacy.

Ostensible differences between spices and other luxury commodities break down before the evidence of their consistent representation as aspects of capitalist panegyrics and culinary encomia. Cultural historians of spice have often tried to establish clean temporal and categorical demarcations in these areas, yet this often simply leads to reinventing the wheel by pointing out distinctions between medieval and modern in terms of phenomenological distinctions between spices, coffee and chocolate (for example, Schivelbusch, 3–14). This is not to deny that distinctions were made between different commodities at different times, and that different cultures employed different kinds of rhetoric. But the rhetoric of long-distance trade is remarkably consistent. For example, Giovanni Battista Roberti (1719–1786), in praise of sugar, wrote in *Le fragole* (1752):

> 'From Virginia and from Caracas,
> The Moluccas and far Mexico,
> Others wait for cinnamon,
> Vanilla, cocoa and carnations;
> And that which modern noses yearn,
> Like Helen searching for Menelaus,
> Powder from Brazil and Havana,
> Soft, subtle and sweetly scented.' (In Camporesi, 158)

The topos of products of the world wafting towards the Bolognese sensorium resembles Blackmore. In *Il mondo creato diviso nelle sette giornate* (1686), Father Guiseppe Girolamo Semenzi of the University of Pavia wrote:

> 'The Indian ship carries to European lips
> The sugars of Brazil, the nuts of Banda,
> And strong-smelling goods originating from
> The Moluccas, Ceylon and other strange shores.'
> (In Camporesi, 112)

He also warned of the dangers of the '"Indian broth"' of chocolate, which could inflame the blood too much and create a state of appetite in which '"taste turns remedy to poison"' (in Camporesi, 112). The tropologically unstable aspect of this rhetoric is hard to miss, this time in the context of chocolate. Piero Camporesi describes a new Enlightenment taste for delicate rather than powerful flavours, such as chocolate with a light dusting of vanilla and cinnamon, and delicacies prepared with great difficulty, such as jasmine chocolate. It is evident, however, that the 'global' ideologies of long-distance trade tended to provide a long-lasting framework for these cultural highlights. Lorenzo Magalotti (1637–1703) worked in didactic and panegyric genres, translating John Philips' *Cyder* and attempting the first Italian translation of *Paradise Lost*. He employed the topos of the spicy Zephyr in a poem about drinking chocolate from *Lettere sopra le terre odorose d'Europa e d'America dette volgarmente buccheri* (1695):

> 'You feel running through your veins
> The rush of wind from a fan and bellows,
> As if the Zephyr hard was blowing
> Fully throated through your lips:
> As if its breath was bringing you
> All the western drugs from sunrise:
> Balsam, bezoar and, melted, drenched,
> Several tears of rich quinquina:
> Soconosco, Guatemala's source of wealth.
> And also, . . .
> . . .
>   each and every
> Perfume of the Orient,
> The rivers of the mosques and harems
> And all is fetched to noble lungs
> As to a precious gold alembic,
> And in a fresh new style's distilled,
> The twinning treasure of East and West.'
>
> (In Camporesi, 74–75)

The 'new style' is expressed through rather old styles, in which aristocratic taste becomes an alchemical vessel for the transformation of the raw materials of orientalism into the pure gold of European cultural capital.

Dryden is particularly useful for the argument that the trade winds topos was a persistent example of a capitalist poetics which transcended local differences of politics and style. For in the long history which encompasses Milton and Shelley, it is Dryden (1631–1700) who stands out as the strongest proponent of such a poetics. *Annus Mirabilis* (1667) shows him to be a poet of the mercantilist emporium and of expanding imperial trade interests. Despite the decline in the vogue for pepper after 1650, war with the Dutch and their massacre of British merchants and their Japanese agents at Amboyna inspired Dryden to write a play, *Amboyna* (1673), and *Annus Mirabilis*. Like the prose of contemporary economists such as Barbon, mercantilist poetics helped to neutralize the moral taint of luxury, and to reinvent the trade winds topos as a figure for trade supported by nature and providence.

There is little doubt about the Satanic register of Dryden's figurative attempt to out-Dutch the Dutch. Dryden appears to support the naked opportunism which characterizes their trade. *Annus Mirabilis* contains an account of the interruption at Bergen of a Dutch spice fleet from India, in which the Dutch, described as 'perfum'd prey' (106) are killed by luxury commodities:

> Amidst whole heaps of Spices lights a Ball,
> And now their Odours arm'd against them flie:
> Some preciously by shatter'd Porc'lain fall,
> And some by Aromatick splinters die. (113–116)

This passage was found somewhat ridiculous by Samuel Johnson, and the entire poem was criticized as too full of conceits like this by Scott (Dryden ed. Kinsley and Kinsley, 295, 389–91). However, an anonymous contemporary pamphlet (1673) praised *Annus Mirabilis* as if poetry was both trade and plunder, and Dryden a merchant adventurer in poetics (Dryden ed. Kinsley and Kinsley, 62–63). The linguistic register is a poetically just echo of the ways in which the Dutch torture the English in *Amboyna* (V.i.145–47, 360–62). There, burning matches placed on the fingernails are associated with hot nutmegs. The Dutch are described as 'Castors' or hunted beavers, from whose sacs a perfume is obtained (Dryden ed. Hooker and Swedenberg, I.285). Besides showing the Dutch to be hoist by their own spicy petard, the lines convey the fetishistic, self-moving power of the commodities over their consumers, rising up as if in revenge against too luxurious an appetite. To play with spice is to play with fire: to risk the object becoming more powerful than the subject who assumes he or she is in control of his or her own desires.

The commodities circulated in the East Indian trade are figured as fixed raw material, capable of plunder as simple as the plucking of Eden's forbidden fruit. The East Indies are a zone 'Where wealth, like fruit on precipices, grew, / Not to be gather'd but by Birds of Prey' (43–44). The dialectic between restriction or territory and flow or deterritorialization is here expressed in combative terms. The large structure of the poem gradually accumulates, hardens and fixes spice in place within the processes of imperialism. The early contemplation of trade's fluidity, mediated through natural law theory, was only a gambit to get the figurative movement started.

Flow is justifiable only if it is in a certain direction, towards a certain territory. London becomes the territory into which the flows of spice, perfume and porcelain are concentrated: an emporium of luxury (see stanzas 3, 5, 11, 293, 298, 302, 304). It is imaged as the final resting-place of 'The vent'rous Merchant' (1197), a happy play on words which suggests both adventure, the 'venting' of trade and the Merchant Adventurers' Company. Stanzas 297–98 celebrate the 'silver Thames' (1189), a revision of Spenser which was in turn revised by Blake, in 'London', whose early draft contemplated the 'dirty Thames' and later the 'chartered Thames' (2; see Blake ed. Johnson and Grant, 53; see Erdman, 81). Dryden's Thames is a veritable 'domestick Floud' of prosperity (1189). The final stanza proclaims 'Thus to the Eastern wealth through storms we go' (1213), figuring trade as better for profit than sheer piracy. By the end of the poem, the free trade discussed by writers like Grotius has become the imperial *pax Britannica* of a 'British Ocean' (stanza 302). The final two lines again echo the providentialism of Grotius (Grotius, 5, 8, 63; see Weinbrot, 237–75): 'A constant Trade-wind will securely blow, / And gently lay us on the Spicy shore' (1215–16).

The natural history of the spice islands had interested writers since their discovery, but in the late eighteenth century, it began to be employed in ways which went beyond the medicinal hagiography of precious plants. In the middle of the third canto of *The Loves of the Plants* (1789) Erasmus Darwin comments on the devastation caused by a certain Javan tree. The Upas, or Poison Tree, devastates its environment:

> Where seas of glass with gay reflections smile
> Round the green coasts of Java's palmy isle;
> A spacious plain extends its upland scene,
> Rocks rise on rocks, and fountains gush between;
> Soft zephyrs blow, eternal summers reign,
> And showers prolific bless the soil, – in vain!
> – No spicy nutmeg scents the vernal glades,
> Nor towering plaintain [sic] shades the mid-day vales;
> No grassy mantle hides the sable hills,
> No flowery chaplet crowns the trickling rills
> . . .
> Fierce in the dread silence on the blasted heath
> Fell UPAS sits the HYDRA-TREE of death.   (II.iii.219–38)

Despite its decline in status as a luxury commodity, nutmeg is still imaged in Darwin as a delicious aspect of a terrestrial paradise, an eternal season where zephyrs blow, the harbingers of spring, and the spice makes the gales fragrant in all their 'vernal', spring-like beauty; Darwin's use of 'eternal summers' may simply be an unfortunate debt to correct scansion. But the 'blasted heath', an allusion to *Macbeth*, reconfigures the Edenic island as a space of death, in a grotesque juxtaposition of Shakespeare's Scottish landscape with the East Indies.

It is strange, then, that Percy Bysshe Shelley (1792–1822), in his sophisticated radical allegory *Queen Mab* (1813), would figure commercial activity as the Upas tree, deriving his image from this section of Darwin's poem, given that the tree is what appears to devastate the trade in nutmeg which made Java famous, along with its coffee trade:

> Commerce! beneath whose poison-breathing shade
> No solitary virtue dares to spring;
> But poverty and wealth with equal hand
> Scatter their withering curses, and unfold
> The doors of premature and violent death,
> To pining famine and full-fed disease,
> To all that shares the lot of human life,
> Which poisoned body and soul, scarce drags the chain,
> That lengthens as it goes and clanks behind. (V.44).

The imagery of lengthening chains was also used in the poetry of anti-slavery, which sought metonymically to relate sugar, the blood of slaves and the British consumer, for example, in Hannah More's *Slavery* (1788; 103).

The images of the poison tree's scattered leaves, and the lengthening chain express the sense of evil circulation. The effects of commerce extend to cultivated and domesticated nature: not only all humans but 'all that shares the lot of human life' will be 'poisoned'. Shelley's vegetarian writing, and other sections of *Queen Mab*, re-employed the poison-tree image. For example, there is the radicalism of another reference to the Upas tree, echoed in A *Vindication of Natural Diet*: 'Let the axe / Strike at the root, the poison-tree will fall,' he declares, finding the cause of war in aggression (Shelley, IV, 82; c.f. VI, 10, 15; see Morton, 178–79, 218–19). Commerce is thus tropologically unstable: it is part of both nature and culture, representing for Shelley a faulty circulation in the social body which is a corruption of its true nature. Shelley's re-employment of Darwin's topos, however, is further complicated by his reintroduction of the spice islands, without the spice trade, as an aspect of his reimagined terrestrial paradise in the utopian eighth section of *Queen Mab*. The logic of poison and cure is figured through the spice trade. Yet it is underpinned by a unitary flow of circulating processes: the wide circle described by the land which the Upas tree poisons, or the circulation of spicy air in the reinvigorated sensorium of the new age.

The Upas tree was also used in Blake's *Songs of Experience*, in 'A Poison Tree', to describe the unfortunate results of repressed anger. Refusing to tell his 'wrath' to his foe, the narrator nurtures his rage, until it becomes objectified and alienated in the world outside his soul. The tree parodies the tree in the Garden of Eden, as his foe steals towards it in the depths of night, eats its deadly fruit, and perishes beneath its shade. The oppressive architecture suggested by the overhanging branches of the tree in Blake's illumination is also hinted at in Shelley's condemnation of commerce's 'poison-breathing shade' (V.44). Shelley's *A Refutation of Deism* (1814) contains a passage about poison. A remarkable piece of devil's advocacy, it imparts the idea that the Christian God could have done things much better. In order to refute Theosophus' anthropocentric criticism of the injustice of Christianity, Eusebes says:

> This whole scheme of things might have been, according to our practical conceptions, more admirable and perfect. Poisons, earthquakes, disease, war, famine and venemous serpents; slavery and persecution are the consequences of certain causes, which according to human judgment might have been dispensed with an [sic; 'in'?] arranging the economy of the globe.
>
> (Shelley, VI, 42–43)

Eusebes means this ironically but Shelley himself invested in the idea. The notion of an economy of the globe, a homeostatic system of regulated flows, has overwhelmed any final, arbitrating signifier to which it could be referred. The 'economy of nature' was an element of the discourse of natural religion which was developed further in Haeckel's notion of ecology in the nineteenth century. The ideal social system would be a kind of 'restricted economy', where what was circulated always returned in some manner to its source. The luxurious squandering of energy would be impossible.

Shelley paints a picture of this kind of economic system as if it were a secular form of Christianity's narratives of Fall and Redemption. Indeed, in his utopia, the lion frolics with the lamb, much as they do in Isaiah 11 and in Milton's Eden (IV.343–44). A good example of redeemed economy is found at the beginning *Queen Mab* VIII:

> The habitable earth is full of bliss;
> Those wastes of frozen billows that were hurled
> By everlasting snow-storms round the poles,
> Where matter dared not vegetate or live,
> But ceaseless frost round the vast solitude
> Bounds its broad zone of stillness, are unloosed;
> And fragrant zephyrs there from spicy isles
> Ruffle the placid ocean-deep, that rolls
> Its broad, bright surge to the sloping sand,
> Whose roar is wakened into echoings sweet
> To murmur through the heaven-breathing groves,
> And melodize with man's blest nature there.   (VIII.58–69)

The Miltonic inverted syntax of the first long clause unlooses the very energies of the planet for the service of a utopian, reformed humanity. Shelley characteristically prefers flow over fixity. The metaphor of 'fragrant zephyrs ... from spicy isles' and the 'heaven-breathing groves' chimes with eighteenth-century panegyrics to the providence of British mercantilism. Shelley is saying that the earth has literally tilted back on its axis and that therefore the flux of the seasons no longer operates, so that the globe is bathed in the warmth of an eternal spring: a radical scientific as well as millenarian hypothesis. The scent of spicy islands and groves is a sign of the providential quality of the subject-position required to smell it: for Blackmore, an expensive seat in the theatre that is English global trade, for Shelley, the outlook of a reformist citizen.

However, Shelley was not unambiguous about the spice trade. In his first vegetarian pamphlet, *A Vindication of Natural Diet* (1813), which is adapted from the notes to the very poem I am discussing, Shelley is highly derogatory about spice. The spice trade, that exemplar of the forces which initiated capitalism in the first place, such as monopolies, long-distance trade, the stimulated taste for the exoticized, is just what is wrong with a transnational economy for Shelley. All that supplementarity is just no good for the moral fibre of the body or the nation.

At the close of the vegetarian note to *Queen Mab* (note 17),

Shelley shortens a story told in Plutarch's vegetarian prose about a Spartan who brings fish to an inn and asks the innkeeper to prepare it. Plutarch criticizes the use of spice as a *trophê*, a deviation from nature:

> But we are so refined in our blood-letting that we term flesh a supplementary food and then we need 'supplements' for the flesh itself, mixing oil, wine, honey, fish paste, vinegar, with Syrian and Arabian spices, as though we were really embalming a corpse for burial. (Plutarch, 995C)

Meat-eating is represented as supplementary to a vegetable diet and thus as unnecessary for nutrition. Meat, moreover, is associated with dietary supplements which both disguise death and prepare for death: in using exotic embalming substances, the consumer is embalming the stomach for an early grave. In addition, spice here would be the supplement of a supplement, in a transumptive role which guarantees its demoted status as sheer trope without referential stability. The discourse of the supplement affects the orientalized flow of spices across the integrity of the Roman imperial boundary. In *A Vindication*, 'sanguinary national disputes' are created through trade wars over 'those multitudinous articles of luxury' such as 'spices from India' or wines, dangerously supplemental commodities (Shelley, VI, 14).

Shelley here contradicted the earliest seventeenth-century theoretical and ideological justifications of long-distance trade. Elizabeth I, Samuel Purchas (1575?–1626) and Thomas Mun all advocated the spending of England's surplus money abroad in the acquisition of goods such a spices, drugs, silks and calico from the East Indies. For Mun international trade is 'the very Touchstone of a kingdomes prosperitie' (Mun in Purchas, 732). Mun links individual and national prudence in this matter, employing the same somatic, moral and economic register as Shelley, but to the opposite effect. Mun deals with the objection that spices are unnecessary by describing them as wholesome and 'comfortable' drugs and flavourings (Mun in Purchas, 733). (It is not easy to make a firm distinction, as some sociologists of the commodity do, between *luxury* and *comfort* here.)

It is impossible to imagine an argument more diametrically opposed to Shelley's vegetarian prose. However, there is a contradiction between *Queen Mab*'s spicy isles and this kind of condemnation. What Shelley criticizes at the level of content, he emulates on the plane of expression. Indeed, it is precisely in the context of a healthy, reinvigorated earth that spices are rather archaically represented. Shelley may therefore be seen as part of a tradition that criticized the use of spices as a form of degrading luxury which undermined the individual and national body. In the sixteenth century, the revolutionary Ulrich von Hütten had attacked spices in a similar mode: '"Down with peppers, saffron and silk!" he cries, "... my dearest wish is that no man who cannot do without pepper should be cured of gout or the French disease". Was boycotting pepper in the struggle against capitalism a way of denouncing or protesting at the power of long-distance trade [asks Braudel]?' (Braudel, II, 418). In Britain, this tradition was directed against French cooking and the long-distance spice trade in the eighteenth century, for example in the medical work of George Cheyne and John Arbuthnot, and by Addison's writing on gluttony, or Steele and Campbell's praise of simplicity against continental tastes amongst wealthy town dwellers (Drummond and Wilbraham, 214–15, 252–54). But Shelley also uses language associated with mercantilist defences of long-distance trade, specifically the spice trade. Nor is it the case that he entirely rejected transumptive or self-reflexive rhetoric. In 'Fragments of an Unfinished Drama', set in 'the Indian archipelago', the Lady, in conversation with the Indian, depicts a strange plant given to her by a spirit in a dream:

> Its shape was such as summer melody
> Of the south wind in spicy vales might give
> To some light cloud bound from the golden dawn
> To fairy isles of evening. (215–18)

Shelley here demonstrates his penchant for hyperreal images which invert what readers expect of similes. Instead of an anticipated concretization of the abstract, he describes an image in terms of something even more evanescent or figural. He is exploiting the utopian register of the oneiric horizon: the lands of spice as the land of dreams and desires, the Hesperides or evening isles (see Le Goff, 230–98). But he is also using spice in a figure about figurality, and in a positive way. The image continues by describing how the plant, mirrorlike, reflects everything around it. This positive valuation of dizzying tropology might seem unexpected from an analysis of other places in his culinary rhetoric. Shelley's ambiguity in this matter may be explained by exploring his vacillation towards capitalism, of which his reformist vegetarian rhetoric is a symptom

(Morton, chapter 6). Shelley wished neatly to divide the drug-poison-trope mode of the pharmacological register from the providence-islands-medicine mode in *Queen Mab*, but the presence of a certain sense of commerce, economy, circulation or flow in both modes contaminated his division. And the role of the spice trade in his vegetarian rhetoric, which is associated with the places in *Queen Mab* where the trade winds topos appears, is negative, supplementary and corrupting, both of the individual body and of the nation. However, despite its many shifting valences, the luxurious quality of spice-as-figure remained, and its role as a literary device persisted.

Conclusion

In conclusion, a number of surprising features emerge. There appear to be no clear distinctions between 'modern' and 'medieval' or premodern representations of spice. The registers of fantasy islands, medicine, festivity, luxury, religious devotion, lust, eroticism and supplementarity, and so on, all continue. It is difficult to draw a line in the sand to mark the commencement of the modern period or of capitalism through the use of spice in literature. It is possible, however, to delineate shifting emphases in these different registers and processes. The ideologies of popular vegetarianism in the eighteenth century, for example, are an obvious instance at which spice becomes, though not for the first time, denigrated as a non-nutritious and ennervating supplement. There is also no clear distinction to be established between 'Augustan' and 'Romantic' representations of the spice trade. In fact, Dryden and Blackmore reaccentuated what I have called its 'Satanic' or mercantile mode, while Darwin and Shelley developed its Edenic and medical modes. The commonly-held assumption that Romanticism in general, and Shelley in particular, augment Milton's representation of Satan, runs aground. The separation of the luxury and medical status of spice depends upon contextual circumstances.

The trade winds topos naturalized trade by showing how the earth was providentially available for the pursuance of trade. Related topoi construed a planet upon which the scattered limbs of humanity could be knitted together by trade. In the preface to the 1598 edition of *Voyages and Discoveries* Hakluyt declared his intention to 'incorporate into one body the torn and scattered limbs' of English trading narratives (Hakluyt, 35). When Elizabeth I wrote to the King of Achen in Sumatra, in the context of the founding of the East India Company (1600), she developed this rhetorical mode (Purchas, I.iii chapter 3, 3.154; see Keay, 11–12). England, naturally, was perceived to be rather better for the Sumatrans in this matter than the Spaniards or Portuguese. This troping of trade continued in the eighteenth century, for instance in George Lillo's *The London Merchant* (1731): trade 'promotes humanity . . . diffusing mutual love from pole to pole' (Lillo, 40). Lillo's phraseology is strikingly similar to Shelley's. Despite local political differences, a certain rhetorical register concerning free trade persisted, which could be named 'antisparagmos': a drive against the fragmentation of the global body of mankind.

The role of a rhetoric about nature, if anything, increased as mercantilism declined and laissez faire capitalism grew in influence, coupled with the rise of imperialism. While Darwin and Shelley wrote, books appeared on the natural history of the islands, and of the West Indies. They smoothed over two hundred years of environmental and social alteration and control with exquisite illustrations of flora and fauna. The genre of the natural history of the East and West Indies could be used subversively: Stedman's magisterial narrative about the slave uprisings in Surinam is a fine example. *Outlines of the Globe* (1798–1800) by the naturalist and traveller Thomas Pennant (1726–1798) contains botanical and proto-anthropological information about the East Indies, and literary quotations from *The Lusiads* and elsewhere. The travel narratives of merchants like Jean Baptiste Tavernier, whom Pennant acknowledges (Pennant, II, 5), which in their turn had supplanted tales of wonder, had given way to natural-historical accounts. Darwin and Shelley employed these new figures. Yet, however natural the islands now begin to seem, they are ultimately the source of the same commodities, and are described as such. These phenomena should alert the historian to the impossibility of accounting for the persistence of the spice trade in English literature as the effect of a superstructural lag.

The continued use of spices in literary topoi relative to their shifting status in consumption and long-distance trade should warn us of the relative autonomy of literary language in its contact with political issues. The trade winds topos is a form of advertising language, to a certain extent. It encourages the pleasurable consumption not only of images of delicious food, but also of images of commercial activity itself. This is one sense in which its poetics is related to various political agenda associated with capitalism. The aesthetics of spice is not static, to use the terminology of Stephen Dedalus in Joyce's A *Portrait of the Artist as a Young Man*, but kinetic, head-turning: it uses turns of phrase to advert our gaze. Dryden's rhetoric of spice seems most clearly designed to fulfil this mission. Shelley's vegetarian rhetoric is often diametrically opposed to this kind of capitalist poetics: it is aversive, rather than advertising, designed to turn the head away. As Jennifer Wicke, however, says of advertisements: 'advertising does not serve as a simple messenger-boy of ideology, if only because ideology does not exist in some place apart before it is channeled through advertisement. The richness of advertisement as a cultural structure ... ensures that [it] ... will not, and cannot, wither away' (Wicke, 16). The discourse of the trade winds topos, like advertising, is 'self-referential and excessive', for it 'relates ... the ongoing surplus, the extra that must be deployed in aesthetic form to reveal itself within the social world as a surplus' (Wicke, 174–75).

This project was supported in part by a New York University Research Challenge Fund Grant. I would like to thank Carol Urness, Brad Oftelie and Brian Hanson of the James Ford Bell Library, University of Minnesota, for their assistance.

References

Appadurai, Arjun, ed., *The Social Life of Things: Commodities in Cultural Perspective* (Cambridge: Cambridge University Press, 1986).
Appleby, Joyce Oldham, *Economic Thought and Ideology in Seventeenth-Century England* (Princeton: Princeton University Press, 1976).
Blackmore, Richard, *Creation. A Philosophical Poem. Demonstrating the Existence and Providence of a God. In Seven Books*, second edn. (London: printed for S. Buckley and J. Tonson, 1712).
Blake, William, *Blake's Poetry and Designs*, ed. Johnson, Mary Lynn and Grant, John E. (London and New York: Norton, 1979).
Braudel, Fernand, *Civilization and Capitalism, 15th–18th Century*, tr. Reynolds, S., 3 vols. (Berkeley and Los Angeles: University of California Press, 1982–84).
Camporesi, Piero, *Exotic Brew: the Art of Living in the Age of Enlightenment*, tr. Woodall, Christopher (Oxford, Cambridge and Cambridge, Mass: Polity Press, 1994).

Darwin, Erasmus, *The Botanic Garden; a Poem, in Two Parts* (London: printed for J. Johnson, 1791).
Diodorus Siculus, *Diodori Siculi bibliothecæ historicæ libri xv. hoc est, quotquot Græce extant, de quadraginta. quorum quinque nunc primum Latine eduntur, de quibus in præstione edoceberis. Adiecta his sunt ex iis libris qui non extant, fragmenta quaedam. Sebastiano Castalione totius operis correctore, partim interprete. Præterea interiecta est Dictys Cretensis & Daretis Phrygii de bello Troiano historia, ad supplendam lacunam quinque librorum, qui inter quintum & undecimum desiderantur* (Basileæ: per H. Petri, 1559).
Dodge, Ernest S., *Islands and Empires: Western Impact on the Pacific and East Asia* (Minneapolis: University of Minnesota Press, 1976).
Drummond, J.C. and Wilbraham, A., *The Englishman's Food: a History of Five Centuries of English Diet* (London: Jonathan Cape, 1939; repr. Pimlico, 1991).
Dryden, John, *The Works of John Dryden*, ed. Hooker, Edward Niles and Swedenberg, H.T., vol. I (Berkeley and Los Angeles: University of California Press, 1961).
Dryden: the Critical Heritage, ed. Kinsley, James and Kinsley, Helen (New York: Barnes and Noble, 1971).
Gilman, Ernest B., 'Madagascar on My Mind: Van Dyck, Arundel, Junius and the Arts of Colonization', paper given at the New York University Seminar on the Renaissance, 28 March 1995.
Grotius, Hugo, *The freedom of the seas; or, the Right which Belongs to the Dutch to Take Part in the East Indian Trade*, tr. Magoffin, Ralph Van Deman (Oxford and New York: Oxford University Press, 1916).
Hakluyt, Richard, *Voyages and Discoveries: the Principal Navigations, Voyages, Traffiques and Discoveries of the English Nation*, ed. Beeching, Jack (London: Penguin, 1972; repr. 1985).
Helgerson, Richard, *Forms of Nationhood: the Elizabethan Writing of England* (Chicago and London: University of Chicago Press, 1992; paperback 1994).
Keay, John, *The Honourable Company: a History of the East India Company* (Oxford, New York and Toronto: Macmillan, 1991).
Le Goff, Jacques, *Pour un autre Moyen Age: temps, travail et culture en Occident* (Paris: Editions Gallimard, 1977).
Lillo, George, *The London Merchant* (1731), ed. William H. McBurney (Lincoln and London: University of Nebraska Press, 1965).
Milton, John, *Paradise Lost*, ed. Fowler, Alastair (London and New York: Longman, 1968, 1971).
John Milton: Complete Shorter Poems, ed. Carey, John (London and New York: Longman, 1968, 1971).
Monardes, Nicolás, *Ioyfull Newes out of the New-found Worlde. Wherein are Declared, the Rare and Singular Vertues of Diuers Herbs, Trees, Plantes, Oyles & Stones, with their Applications, as well to the Use of Phisicke, as of Chirurgery: which being well Applyed, Bring such Present Remedie for all Diseases, as may Seem altogether Incredible: notwithstanding by Practice found out to be True*, tr. Frampton, John (London: printed by E. Allde, 1596).
Montanari, Massimo, *The Culture of Food*, tr. Ipsen, Carl (Oxford and Cambridge, Mass.: Basil Blackwell, 1994).
More, Hannah, *Slavery, a Poem* (London: printed for T. Cadell, 1788).
Morton, Timothy, *Shelley and the Revolution in Taste: the Body and the Natural*

World (Cambridge and New York: Cambridge University Press, 1994).
Pennant, Thomas, Outlines of the Globe, 4 vols. (London: Henry Hughes and Luke Hansard, 1798–1800).
Plutarch, Plutarch's Moralia, tr. Cherniss, H. and Helbold, W.C., vol. XII (London: William Heinemann and Cambridge, Mass: Harvard University Press, 1957).
Purchas, Samuel, Purchas his Pilgrimes. In Five Bookes, 4 vols. (London: printed for Henry Fetherstone, 1625).
Schivelbusch, Wolfgang, Tastes of Paradise: a Social History of Spices, Stimulants, and Intoxicants (New York: Pantheon, 1992).
Shakespeare, William, Hamlet, Prince of Denmark, ed. Edwards, Philip (Cambridge: Cambridge University Press, 1985; repr. 1993).
Othello, ed. Sanders, Norman (Cambridge: Cambridge University Press, 1984; repr. 1993).
Macbeth, ed. Muir, Kenneth (London and New York: Methuen, 1951; repr. 1982).
Shelley, Percy Bysshe, The Complete Works, ed. Ingpen, R. and Peck, W.E., 10 vols. (London and New York: Ernest Benn, 1926–30).
Smith, Nigel, Literature and Revolution in England, 1640–1660 (New Haven and London: Yale University Press, 1994).
Tavernier, Jean Baptiste, The Six Voyages of John Baptista Tavernier, a Noble Man of France now Living, through Turky [sic] into Persia, and the East-Indies, Finished in the Year 1670, Giving an Account of the State of those Countries. Together with a New Relation of the Present Grand Seignor's Seraglio, by the Same Author. To Which is Added a Description of all the Kingdoms which Encompass the Euxine and Caspian Seas. By an English Traveller, Never Before Printed, tr. Phillips, John (London: printed for 'R.L.' and 'M.P.', 1678).
Thomson, James, The Seasons and the Castle of Indolence, ed. Sambrook, James (Oxford: the Clarendon Press, 1972; repr. 1989).
Weinbrot, Howard D., Britannia's Issue: the Rise of British Literature from Dryden to Ossian (Cambridge and New York: Cambridge University Press, 1993).
Wicke, Jennifer, Advertising Fictions: Literature, Advertisement, and Social Reading (New York: Columbia University Press, 1988).

Island Queens: Nationalism, Queenliness and Women's Poetry 1837–1861

HELEN GROTH

THE DEATH OF William IV on 20th June 1837 ushered in the long expected reign of Queen Victoria. Elizabeth Barrett opens her poem *The Young Queen* with a quotation from 'The Queen's Declaration in Council' delivered on the day of Victoria's official accession to the throne: 'This awful responsibility is imposed upon me so suddenly, and at so early a period of my life, that I should feel myself utterly oppressed by the burden, were I not sustained by the hope that Divine Providence, which has called me to this work, will give me strength for the performance of it' (1904, 315). Victoria's protestations decorously balance her youthful and humble anxieties concerning her new role, the weight of her grief, and her exemplary faith in God's will, with an underlying confidence in her ability to fulfil her duty to her nation. Elizabeth Barrett's fascination with the lachrymose yet professionally confident image of Victoria's accession is registered by the devotion of a second poem to the subject, *Victoria's Tears*. These poems were published during July 1837, less than a month after they were written, in the *Athenaeum*, the *Reading Mercury*, the *Oxford Gazette* and *Berkshire County Paper*. The speed of the poems' publication and their publishing context in a periodical, a gazette and two newspapers, reflects the topicality of their subject.

In a letter to her friend Mary Russell Mitford, Elizabeth Barrett expresses her fascination with Victoria:

> I am sure I ought to be proud of my verses finding their way into a Belford Reg's Newspaper! The young Queen is very interesting to me – and those tears, wept not only amidst the multitudes at the proclamation, but in the silence of the dead midnight – (we heard that she cried all night before holding her first Privy Council, notwithstanding the stateliness and composure with which she received her councillors) – are beautiful and touching to think upon ... There is something hardening, I fear, in power – even if there is not in pomp! and the coldness of state etiquette gather too nearly around the heart, not to chill it, very often. But our young Queen

wears still a very tender heart – and long may its natural emotions lie warm within it. (Miller, 1959, 16)

Victoria's spectacular display of grief in the domain of politics, as well as 'in the silence of the dead of night', destabilises the boundary between public and private spheres. The Queen is a hybrid figure in Barrett's poems and correspondence, a professional Victorian woman. Victoria answers the call of her genealogically determined vocation. Her duty is a public one, just like the woman poet in Barrett's work, who must fulfil her god-given task, even when the personal cost is the display of sentiment in a public, rather than a private place.

The connection between the young Queen and the woman poet is explicitly made in Henry Chorley's announcement in the *Athenaeum* on Saturday June 1st 1850, that Elizabeth Barrett Browning was the most suitable candidate to fill Wordsworth's place as Laureate:

> There is more than one worthy recipient of the laurel, – and more than one, unhappily, the state of whose fortunes makes it needful that the leaves should be gilded. But we cannot help suggesting that in the reign of a youthful Queen, if there be among her subjects one of her own sex whom the laurel will suit, its grant to a female would be at once an honourable testimonial to the individual, a fitting recognition of the remarkable place which the women of England have taken in the literature of the day, and a graceful compliment to the sovereign herself. It happens to fall in well with this view of the case, that there is no living poet, of either sex who can prefer a higher claim than Mrs Elizabeth Barrett Browning.
> (Chorley, 1850, 585)

Critics have read this announcement as a symbolically inclusive gesture towards women writers excluded by an impenetrable literary establishment (Leighton, 1992; Cooper, 1988). A consideration of the context of the announcement complicates this reading. The status of the crown of laurel was questionable for Chorley. His announcement opens with a call to be 'rid of the mummeries of the Laureateship', echoing previous demands for its abolition made in the *Athenaeum* and *The Times*. On April 27th 1850 the Laureateship is described by the *Athenaeum* as 'a merely nominal office, whose duties belong to the time of court jesters, and were of even less dignity and value than theirs. When the title had any meaning at all, it presented the poet in the character of a parasite'. Instead of the anachronistically 'offensive title' the establishment of a pension to be awarded to the most worthy candidate is suggested as a more practical and modern alternative. Inherent in these demands and Chorley's announcement is a desire to professionalise and modernise the role of the poet in society. Financial need coupled with ability replace decadent aristocratic tradition. Elizabeth Barrett Browning fulfils the requirements of this 'poetic middle-class entrepreneurial spirit' (Cooper, 1988, 9). Tennyson was an unpopular choice in the opinion of the *Athenaeum* critics, as his appointment seemed to champion the elitist nostalgia they felt had had its day. However, Chorley's sceptical attitude to aristocratic tradition is undermined by his explicit linkage of the new Queen and Elizabeth Barrett Browning as the suitable poet laureate and by Barrett Browning's own identification and fascination with the rituals of monarchic tradition in her representations of Victoria.

Elizabeth Barrett's interest in the self concealed behind the ritualised mask of the new Queen was also shared by other Victorian women. This interest is signalled by the plethora of often sensational biographies of Victoria by women during her reign. The most famous of these was Agnes Strickland's heavily censored biography *Queen Victoria, from Birth to Bridal*. Victoria's copy of this biography, which she read after its publication, is covered with marginalia correcting Strickland's representation of her childhood and adolescence (Woodham Smith, 1972, 30). There are also numerous poems by women celebrating the public events of Victoria's life and many more which invoke the metaphor of queenliness to interrogate the boundaries of both poetic and English national identity. Five poems representing specific historical occasions in Victoria's life from 1837 to 1861 will form the frame for this analysis of the pervasive presence of the concept of queenliness in Victorian women's poetry; Elizabeth Barrett's *The Young Queen* and *Victoria's Tears*, Christina Rossetti's *The Mourning Queen* and two poems which serve as a context for Barrett's and Rossetti's interest in Victoria and queenliness, Sara Ellis' *The Island Queen* and Caroline Norton's *The Chapel Royal, on the 10th February, 1840*.

Victoria and Albert became icons of an idealised myth of English national character. They occupied a central place in a familial tableaux which recurred obsessively in the journalism, literature, art and popular memorabilia of the period. Women poets' identification with Victoria reflects the necessary fragmentation of an idealised subject, selectively interpreted and rendered incoherent by the variable symbolic investments of the reader. The representation of Queen Victoria by women poets raises a range of complex questions concerning the relation between gender and authority, monarchism, race and the construction of national narratives in Victorian culture. These women did not respond to Victoria in the same way. Thus, it is difficult to extrapolate from the poems a generalised account of how women identified with Victoria. These texts reveal the inherent contradictions in the female subject within Victorian culture and the untenability of constructing a distilled opposition between women and monolithic systems of power. The poems this chapter will discuss exemplify the differences between middle class women poets' perception of Victoria, complicating a simple dichotomous picture of women identifying with their Queen as part of a narrative of female assertiveness or domestic submission.

If Victoria is a figure of power, the power she represents is an ambivalent one, an ambivalence reflected in Victoria's own correspondence and diary. In a letter to Gladstone opposing the indecency of women studying with men to be doctors, Victoria acknowledges the anomalous nature of her position: 'The Queen is a woman – herself – and knows what an anomaly her *own* position is – but that can be reconciled with reason and propriety tho' it is a terribly difficult and trying one' (Guedalla, 1934, 271–2). Yet, as Elisabeth Helsinger observes, even though Victoria excoriated women's rights issues her orthodoxy is not coherently unproblematic (1983, 1: 63). Her correspondence reflects both her discomfort with political life and her unease concerning Albert's growing interests in public matters: 'Albert grows daily fonder and fonder of politics and business and is so wonderfully *fit* for both – such perspicacity and such *courage* – I grow daily to dislike them both more and more ... Albert becomes really a *terrible* man of business; I think it takes a little off from the gentleness of his character, and makes him so preoccupied. I grieve over all this, as I *cannot* enjoy these things, *much* as I interest myself in *general* European politics; but I am everyday more convinced that *we women*, if we *are* to be *good* women, *feminine* and *amiable* and *domestic*, are *not fitted to reign*;... However this cannot now be helped, and it is the duty of everyone to fulfil all that they are called upon to do, in whatever situation they may be!' (Benson and Esher, 1907, 2: 438–44). The peremptory tone of the final line forecloses on Victoria's seemingly overwhelming anxieties concerning her public duties. She must take up her position in the public sphere as destiny decrees.

Regardless of Victoria's affected political reticence many women focused on this facet of her identity. H.G. Wells records his mother's memory of the accession of Victoria as an act of political identification: 'I do not think it is on record anywhere, but it is plain to me from what I have heard my mother say, that among school-mistresses and such like women at any rate, there was a stir of emancipation associated with the claim of the Princess Victoria... to succeed King William IV. There was a movement against that young lady based on her sex and this provoked in reaction a wave of feminine partisanship throughout the country' (Hardie, 1935, 140). Historians have observed that the Queen Caroline affair had caused similar outrage amongst women in Britain leading to a growth in popular literature, comprising both poems and tracts protesting against her unfair treatment (Colley, 1992; Davidoff and Hall, 1994). Elizabeth Barrett participated in this national concern for Caroline, dramatising the Queen's woes at the hands of an unjustly cruel King in an unpublished dialogue between Caroline and her daughter Charlotte (Buxton Forman, 1914, 1: 148–62). Princess Charlotte's death represented, for many, the tragic end of their hopes for a rejuvenated monarchy. Women were prominent in the expression of this general woe over the loss of Charlotte, with whom Victoria was commonly compared, thus establishing a precedent for women's intense political identification with royal women.

Women poets made Victoria the repository for a range of narratives; professional, domestic, religious and national. Victoria functions as a palimpsest for these poets; a complexly layered body emblematizing 'common values', such as maternal love, wifely duty and national pride. The monarchy is invoked in all these poems to signify the maintenance of social order and its attendant hierarchies, even while both the material and ideological boundaries of what constitutes the duty and identity of a queen are being interrogated. David Gervais in his recent study *Literary Englands* defends his omission of English women writers by claiming that when he thought of including them he 'began to wonder if their concern with "Englishness" were not of a different order, perhaps less geared by nationalistic feelings' (1993, xii). In contrast to Gervais' assumption, women poets exploited a patriotic and poetic mode also employed by Tennyson as Laureate, in poems such as *On The Jubilee of Queen Victoria* and the epilogue to *The Idylls of The King* (Ricks, 1969, 1369). Elizabeth Barrett early in her career, in the preface to

The Battle of Marathon, explicitly linked the act of writing poetry to patriotic virtue. Women's poems resemble Tennyson's official poetry as Laureate in their compulsion to extrapolate a unified idea of nation as a symbolic force and superimpose this idea onto the body of Victoria. John Lucas, in his analysis of the Victorians and patriotism, elucidates this process: 'Patriotism – love of England – meant almost exclusively love of England as embodied in and by Victoria' (1987/8, 63). David Cannadine describes this identification process as 'an anthropomorphic miracle' (1989, 25). Lucas is critical of Cannadine's trivialisation of a much more profound shift from the anti-monarchic feeling, which had been growing during the reigns of Victoria's predecessors, to the creation of England as a quintessentially Victorian and 'royalist nation' during Victoria's reign. Lucas convincingly traces this transformation through the analysis of the creation of Victoria as a bourgeois icon by the deliberate muting of the autocratic associations with monarchy and the foregrounding of the link between Victoria and liberty.

My own analysis of the 'loved body' of Victoria departs from Lucas at the point where he excludes women from the process of identifying with Victoria in any way other than through the frame of domestic ideology: '. . . a complex female figure is produced as the emblem of England and of what is identified as English values. Moreover, this loved body is largely put together by and for male consumption. (Victorian patriotism had little to offer women beyond their being encouraged to develop as images of the queen, in whose sign husbands might conquer)' (1987/8, 65). A more accurate and politically telling formulation might have been, that the loved body of Victoria was put together by and for bourgeois consumption by both sexes, with an underlying agenda of suppressing differences within the British Isles and striving to make England and Britain interchangeable terms. Middle class poets of both genders catered to their middle class readers' fascination with the aristocracy. Geoffrey Best attributes the irresistible fascination with the aristocracy of 'a historically – and hierarchically minded, socially ambitious and envious society' to a nostalgic desire for the heroic. The aristocracy 'were supposed to look handsomer, love more passionately and behave more impressively than lower-bred mortals' (1979, 266). Alan Sinfield is more damning in his portrayal of the closed society produced by this hierarchical symbolic identification: 'This was the pinnacle of the pyramid of deference which kept most Victorians from aspiring too far above their places. Despite the vigour with which the bourgeois dominated industrial and commercial relations and imposed their culture on the nation, they retained as a glittering instance of true nobility the idea of aristocratic birth' (Sinfield, 1986, 162).

Lucas assumes that only men had the hegemonic control to produce a concept of nationhood, which in the case of Sarah Ellis, one of the most popular domestic ideologues of the 1830s and 1840s, is clearly incorrect. Ellis explicitly links her pedagogic work to Victoria in her dedication of her enormously popular *The Wives of England* to her sovereign. Her representation of Victoria in *The Island Queen* is characterised by a complex set of narratives simultaneously tied to the compulsion to produce a seamless image of nationhood, a strong religious mission, domestic ideology, francophobia (and the implicit anti-Republicanism that brought with it), and an idea of queenliness as the apotheosis of English liberty. Ellis ties this representation to a progressive view of history as an unfolding process moving towards a sublime goal which, for Ellis, is ultimately the service of God.

I. Islands and Queens

Ellis defines *The Island Queen* as a political tract in verse form. She asks her readers to 'Blame not the verse' as it is merely a conduit rendered transparent by the poem's glorious mission to celebrate those who pursue 'an embassy of Christian love', an embassy not to the powerful and fashionable but 'To the savage in his mountain cave' (1846, 27). Ellis sees *The Island Queen* as an historically contingent speech act which is given meaning by the political and religious context which informs it, rather than as an aesthetic artefact. Its literary value lies in its political effectiveness as a persuasive document which encourages its readers to pursue a Christian mission to save Tahiti; whether the reader was Queen Victoria, to whom the poem is explicitly addressed, or the members of the London Missionary Society, of which Sarah Ellis and her husband William were active participants.

For Ellis, Victoria is a young Queen surrounded by potentially corrupt advisors who needs to be persuaded to embark on a glorious mission to save the beleaguered Queen of Tahiti, Pomare, whose country was taken from her by the French. Until this point, there had been no attempts to colonise Tahiti, even though as Anthony

Pagden notes, the eighteenth century explorer Louis Antoine Bougainville discovered Tahiti leaving behind a plaque bearing the title 'This land is ours' (1993, 137). British missionaries had arrived in 1797 and succeeded in converting Queen Pomare's predecessors, but Tahiti itself was not seen as an English colony. In 1836 French missionaries attempted to open a mission. Queen Pomare, on the advice of the English missionaries expelled them, leading to the arrival of a French frigate in 1838 demanding recompense and the right of settlement for the French. Pomare appealed unsuccessfully to England for assistance: the lack of this assistance led to her forced signing over of the islands to French control in 1843. Pomare was deposed and though England protested against her unjust treatment, no direct intervention was made to protect Tahiti from French colonisation. Both *The Times* and the *Illustrated London News* published extensive reports of the parliamentary debates between Sir Charles Napier and Sir Robert Peel over the 'French Outrages in Tahiti' (1844, 3; 1844, 66). Napier describes the fate of Tahiti as a 'question of some importance to the character and honour of the British Nation'. The extent of interest in the matter is registered by Barrett Browning's reference to Pomare in *Aurora Leigh*, twelve years after the furore had died down. (Kaplan, 1978, 5:823) Lord Howe's playful description of a besotted reader's desire for Aurora Leigh's autograph aligns the poet's celebrity with Pomare's:

> I saw you across the room, and stayed, Miss Leigh,
> To keep a crowd of lion-hunters off,
> With faces toward your jungle. There were three;
> A spacious lady, five feet ten and fat,
> Who has the devil in her (and there's room)
> For walking to and fro upon the earth,
> From Chipewa to China; she requires
> Your autograph upon a tinted leaf
> 'Twixt Queen Pomare's and Emperor Soulouque's.

Pomare, like Aurora, is merely one of a list of exotic names signifying the conventionally eccentric woman traveller's voracious desire to move across foreign topographies collecting trophies as she goes.

In contrast to the dilettantism of Barrett Browning's lady traveller, Ellis is profoundly opposed to French colonisation, which she sees as Catholic, republican and economically motivated. She represents it as an act of violation of a 'mother and a queen' and a potentially analogic violation of Victoria, if the French had chosen England and not Tahiti to invade. Tahiti, in Ellis' eyes, had become another England under the guidance of the missionaries; a garden of virtuous labour peopled with anglicised Tahitians who mirror the English in moral characteristics. Pomare, their Queen, is a 'savage' double for Victoria. Ellis' description of Pomare's accession and wedding closely resemble Caroline Norton's adulatory descriptions of Victoria's wedding, which will be discussed later in this chapter. The Island Queen, like Victoria, is the focus of a nation's gaze, her body, like Victoria's, blurring with the nation she leads. Barrett Browning performs a similar 'anthropomorphic miracle', to invoke Cannadine's words, in the second part of *Casa Guidi Windows* in which she portrays England as a queen drawing in her robes in her sceptical description of the imperial grandeur of the Crystal Palace Exhibition in which materialism is celebrated at the expense of the poor and politically disenfranchised;

> But now, the world is busy; it has grown
> A Fair-going world. Imperial England draws
> The flowing ends of the earth, from Fez, Canton,
> Delhi and Stockholm, Athens and Madrid,
> The Russias and the vast Americas,
> As if a queen drew in her robes amid
> Her golden cincture, – isles, peninsulas,
> Capes, continents, fair inland countries hid
> By jasper-sands and hills of chrysopras,
> All trailing in their splendours through the door
> Of the gorgeous Crystal Palace ...   (1904, 370)

Empire is a garment which the imperial centre draws towards her when she so desires. Different cultures' wares are transfigured into jewels in England's crown to be displayed and sold to the highest bidder in the marketplace of gold and glass, the Crystal Palace. The poem's speaker registers her disgust with the over-valuing of the 'golden cincture' of material objects of desire, regardless of their beauty, at the expense of the moral duty of 'liberal nations' to the disenfranchised people within the boundaries of their various empires. England is reminded of its duty to the 'wicked children' it has failed to educate and the 'women, sobbing out of sight' prostituted and criminalised by laws designed to exact retribution rather than foster compassion. The speaker also confronts Austria with the exiling and oppression of its political dissidents in the wake of the 1848 revolutions, Russia over the treatment of the 'knouted Poles', America over the issue of slavery, and France and Italy are invoked as examples of the continuing political turmoil in Europe which the Crystal Palace Exhibition's celebration of material success and cultural accord wilfully excludes from its narrative of progress.

In a similar, yet more expansive style to Barrett Browning, Sarah Ellis in *The Island Queen* confronts her Queen and the English public with a narrative which she feels has been excluded by moral apathy, as well as political and economic corruption. Ellis believes that it is the power of 'The Word of God' which will encourage Victoria to embark on a mission to save another island Queen and therefore uses the larger part of the poem to detail the glorious achievements of missionary work in Polynesia. *The Island Queen* is a poem, to a large extent, about the transformative power of language. Ellis extols the virtues of literacy throughout the poem:

> Chieftains were proud to follow – books were sought
> E'en aged men the aspiring impulse caught;
> And oft beside the blue sea's peaceful strand,
> The warrior stopped to write upon the sand,
> Tracing faint characters, and soon effaced,
> Yet in their import, ne'er to be erased.   (1846, 89)

To educate the Tahitians is represented as the most noble work and suitable for 'earnest workmen ... Not men who merely shed a seemly tear!'. Barrett Browning in her tirade against the wrongs of 'liberal nations', in *Casa Guidi Windows*, places a similar emphasis on the 'teaching' of those 'Who sit in darkness when it is not night'. For Ellis, missionary work is the only form of virtuous travel and colonisation. Christianisation transforms the listless savage 'with sinews all unstrung' into a socialised individual 'who plants and plans'. In contrast, colonisation only for economic ends decimates 'ancient tribes' and violates the human rights of people deprived of the self-defence of possessing taught minds to deal with Europeans in their own language and on equal ground:

> In all our schemes to civilise mankind
> By planting colonies, this doom we find –
> Extermination – slow, perchance, but sure.
> For how should he, with untaught mind endure
> The tempting snares which on that border-ground
> His steps bewilder, and his path surround?   (1846, 37)

Boundaries between races and the ethical issue of national autonomy are articulated through the politics of language acquisition. Christian pedagogy offers the only model of ethical colonisation: 'Christian love teaches first to feel' and then to survive. Ellis' husband William Ellis spent eight years as a missionary in the Windward and Southsea islands and was the first person to introduce the printing press to Polynesia. On his return to England he published *Polynesian Researches*, which excited great interest and was reviewed by Southey in the *Quarterly Review*. However, Sarah Ellis was William Ellis' second wife and did not accompany him on his travels as his first wife had done. William Ellis plays an important role in *The Island Queen* as a documentary source, cited continuously throughout the poem as empirical proof of the data Ellis uses to describe the wedding of Pomare, at which William Ellis was present, and the pre-Christian rituals of the islanders. William Ellis also appears as a character in the poem to whom the speaker turns for information about Tahiti. Ellis' poem is a compendious discursive text combining theology, ethnography and moral analysis of the ethics of colonisation. Sections of the poem resemble lists accumulating details about the Tahitians' lives referring to lengthy endnotes taken from William Ellis' researches. Sarah Ellis' extensive reproduction of ethnographic data reflects an awareness of cultural differences, even though the text's ultimate goal is to subsume Tahitian rituals into the narrative design of Christian teleology.

As the poem progresses there is an implicit sense of Victoria being taught what Ellis describes as 'moral boldness' through the example of the missionary. This pedagogic aim becomes increasingly explicit in the comparison made between Pomare and Victoria and Tahiti and England. Ellis celebrates the growing chivalry of the 'savages', who she suggests would have fought far afield to protect a defenceless queen, if she was under attack; a suggestion which attempts to create a sense of obligation in Victoria. Ellis celebrates her 'honoured name', 'rank' and 'parentage' and the patriotism of the people, who like the Tahitians, would die to protect their young queen: 'Yes; there are hearts – fair queen – would bleed and burn, / Should injury come thy woman's rights to spurn' (1846, 126–8). Ellis emphasises the inherent fragility and humanity of the royal body of Victoria, which popular feeling guards so zealously: it is a royal body, which in its identity as wife and mother binds 'Alike the queen and peasant' (1846, 129) This analogic connection between Victoria and her subjects again foregrounds her duty to them and levels the stratification of ruler and ruled by making hierarchy contingent on moral duty. The cliché – death or misfortune levels all – informs Ellis' words of advice. Ellis persistently emphasises the tenuousness of national stability which can be so easily threatened from within and without, questioning Victoria in a doubtful tone about her complacence: 'Tread not thy steps as on enchanted ground?'. This destabilisation of smug Englishness culminates in a direct demand that Victoria recognise Pomare as 'one who weeps in exile ... A queen like thee – a wife – a mother too; / Born to a title, like thy birthright true' and an attack on England as the supposed champion of liberty:

> Here lies the stain upon our country's fame;
> Here too begin the first low steps of shame.
> When wealth or luxury forms a nation's boast,
> More deeply than honour gained or lost;   (1846, 140)

Ellis' poem raises important questions about the boundaries between individuals and between nations across which concepts of identity are perpetually being negotiated. (Bhabha, 4) The metaphor of the boundary between public and private spheres embodied in the triune figure of Victoria as mother, wife, and queen also characterises representations of Victoria's coronation and marriage.

II. *Tears, Crowns and Wedding Rings*

In *The Young Queen* Elizabeth Barrett portrays an image of an anxious young Victoria resisting the pomp and ritual of her new role and haunted by the shadow of her dead uncle, William IV. The royal corpse lies unshrouded in the first stanza and the palace and court reverberate with the sounds of weeping courtiers. In the midst of this grief the young queen steps into her rightful place and dons the 'deathly scented crown' (1904, 315). The celebratory spectacle of the coronation forms a backdrop to the psychological drama of Victoria's struggle with grief and her desire for self-concealment; 'Her thoughts are deep within her: / No outward pageants win her'. There is a neurotic edge to the image of Victoria enringed by the 'dust that was a king' standing on the cold earth of 'her father's grave'. The paraphernalia of mourning stifles the young queen, making the memories of her 'childhood's rest ... and sport on grassy sod' difficult to recall. Her body materialises the grief of the nation. She must 'make room within' her 'bright eyes for all its gathered tears' so that 'the grateful isles' can pay her back for the consolation of their grief with loyalty. Victoria's grief is inextricable from her subjects'. Her tears are rhetorically intermingled with theirs.

Barrett repeats the sentiments and images of *The Young Queen* in the more melodramatic *Victoria's Tears*. The staccato rhythm of the poem mirrors the 'the re-iterated clangour' which the poem's epigraph, from Landor's *Gebir*, invokes as the national 'sound' which unites 'all the people', 'From rank to rank' in 'one vast applause' (1904, 316). This is a poem which both describes and perpetuates the myth of national unity. Victoria is addressed as 'O MAIDEN! heir of kings!', whose duty calls her away from her 'mother's breast' to 'rule the land that loves thee best!'. The first stanza closes as it opens, with an exclamation: 'She wept, to wear a crown!'. This line, with minor variations, is the recurring refrain which closes every stanza. Victoria's eyes can be read as transparent surfaces by her subjects communicating a promise of a benign, non-tyrannical reign. The refrain is varied in the poem's closing stanza, as the speaker informs Victoria that she will 'not *weep* / To wear that heavenly crown!'. Victoria's crown has a sublime double with which she will be crowned when death transforms her from mourner to mourned.

Barrett's poem foregrounds both Victoria's genealogy, which makes her a worthy successor to the throne and the ethics of ruling her subjects by manifesting a 'natural' affinity with liberty; and her moral duty to the people who collectively identify with her 'loved body'. Christina Rossetti, like Barrett, insists on the compulsory relation between aristocratic birth and moral obligation to the disenfranchised or dispossessed in *The Royal Princess*, a poem originally published by Emily Faithfull in *Poems: An Offering to Lancashire. Printed and Published for the Art Exhibition for the Relief of Distress in the Cotton Districts* (1863, 2–10). Rossetti's princess is frozen in a hall of mirrors reflecting a self-image overlaid with ritualised and political desires of an administration in which she does not believe. She rails against the suffering of the people over whose bodies the structures of state power are built. Yearning for the 'simplicity' of pastoral bliss, she 'would rather be a peasant with her baby at her breast' than 'lost in mirrors, whereupon I trace/ Self to right hand, self to left hand' until her reflection reveals a face 'old and haggard', shrivelled by the constraints of courtly life (Crump, 1979, 1;149). Confronted with the pain of the workers, she struggles to 'touch my harp' but is distracted by the voices of suffering. Poetry is not enough, direct action must be taken. Finally she is driven from the paralysis of her own lot to descend from her tower, transgressing the decorum of social hierarchy to 'stand face to face' with her suffering subjects. The threat of death is the great leveller of class in Rossetti's text, a moral which aligns her work with Sarah Ellis' foreboding message to Victoria at the close of *The Island Queen*. As Rossetti succinctly states in a much later poem, *Mother Country*;

> Oh what is a handmaid
> Or what is a queen?
> All must lie down together
> Where the turf is green,
> The foulest face hidden,
> The fairest not seen;
> Gone as if never
> They had breathed or been. (Crump, 1979, 1:222)

Though death may be the great leveller, it is birth which is the creator of destined duty in women poets' representations of aristocratic figures. The inherited right to rule is blatantly asserted in Caroline Norton's *The Chapel Royal St James, on The 10th February, 1840*. In contrast to Barrett's portrait of the introspection and neurosis of the pre-coronation Victoria, Norton's text is a celebration of the pomp and display of Victoria's marriage to Albert (1840, 125). Norton gazes patriotically at the spectacle from the position of a privileged insider. Yet, her insider status is not exploited as a means of exploring the psychological drama behind the ritual, but rather her poem reads like the social pages in verse-form. The poem's vision of conjugal bliss and the future breeding of aristocratic stock differs profoundly from Victoria's view of marriage as outlined in a letter to the Princess Royal at the time of the latter's wedding: 'All marriage is such a lottery – the happiness is always an exchange – though it may be a very happy one – still the poor woman is bodily and morally the husband's slave. That always sticks in my throat. When I think of a merry, happy young girl – and look at the ailing, aching state a young wife is generally doomed to – which you can't deny is the penalty of marriage . . . I can't say what I suffered, what

I felt – what struggles I had to go through – (indeed I have not quite got over it yet)' (Fulford, 1964, 254,182, 343).

Norton's poem could be defined in the same terms as Tennyson described *The Queen of The Isles*, which he wrote to commemorate the accession of Victoria and dismissed in a letter to James Spedding as 'newspaper verse' (Ricks, 1969, 95). Norton opens with an image of the popular spectacle of the marriage, with the 'glad expectant faces' of people gathered outside the church to watch the ceremony. Walter Bagehot condemned this mass deference to 'what we may call the *theatrical show* of society . . . a certain pomp of great men; a certain spectacle of beautiful women; a wonderful scene of wealth and enjoyment . . . a certain charmed spectacle which imposes on the many, and guides their fancies at will' (Best, 1979, 259). Bagehot, unlike Norton, was highly conscious of the social travesty concealed beneath the smooth surface of royalist propaganda. In contrast to Bagehot's scepticism, Norton proceeds to ever greater heights of adulation in her celebration of the beauty and pedigree of the Queen's bridesmaids. This prolix sequence of veneration of blood-lines lasts seven stanzas, culminating in the image of Victoria as the apex of this class and breed of female aristocratic stock. Metaphors of breeding are sustained in the representation of Albert as a member of a worthy, yet foreign racial strain who 'from his distant home' has sought 'our island shore'. On arrival Albert gained Victoria and 'England's welcome too' and must therefore 'forget that e'er his harp was strung/ To any accents but our mother-tongue'. Albert's cultural assimilation is articulated in linguistic terms. Erasure of difference is enacted by the removal of all German accents from his voice. National identity becomes a polished veneer which is mobile and easily transposed onto the outward features of a willing subject. The need to remove all public traces of Albert's Germanic stock reflects the anxieties of many English subjects concerning the very German royal family which was meant to embody the supremacy of British sovereignty. The pervasiveness of metaphors of race and breeding indicates the immense ideological value invested in the imaging of the royal family as a pure genetic strain co-extensive with the metonymic figuration of the purity of the English race. It is 'Old England's brightest hopes' which Norton claims are renewed by this royal coupling, firmly tying a chivalric past of good English values and moral order to the iconographic representation of Victoria and Albert. The poem closes with advice to the young Queen not to let the demands of state 'nor tearful thoughts, nor careful thoughts', 'weigh thy spirit down'. Norton blesses Victoria on behalf of her 'loyal subjects'. Yet, the concluding stanzas also register her anxieties about the demands of public life on a young Queen.

Norton's anxieties concerning the Queen's power to balance private emotion with public responsibility are shared by Christina Rossetti in *Our Widowed Queen*, written on December 16th 1861, the day of Albert's death. The poem's title conveys the shared grief of the English nation and their Queen. Rossetti opens with an invocation to God to act as 'Husband', 'Father', 'Friend' and 'Comforter' to Victoria (Crump, 1990, 3: 284). A tolling rhythm, the sustained regular rhyme scheme, and the enumeration of the roles God must now fulfil for the mourning Queen, combine to create a sonorous chanting effect. Rossetti amplifies the virtues of Victoria and Albert's marriage: 'Full twenty years of blameless married faith, / Of love an honour questioned not'. Fidelity and constancy are foregrounded as characteristics of a 'blameless' marriage conveying the exacting nature of the public gaze that judges whether the 'love and honour' of the royal family should be 'questioned not'. *The Times*' report of Albert's death also places fidelity at the centre of its description of the Prince Consort's achievements and expands on the implications of the importance of fidelity to an age concerned as never before with the morals of its rulers and equipped with an ever-enlarging print media to secure those morals; 'The Royal marriage has been blessed with a numerous offspring. So far as it is permitted to the public to know the domestic lives of sovereigns, the people of these islands could set up no better model of the performance of the duties of a wife and mother than their QUEEN; no more complete pattern of a devoted husband and father than her consort. These are not mere words of course. We write in an age and in a country in which the highest position would not have availed to screen the most elevated delinquent. They are simply the records of a truth perfectly understood and recognised by the English people' (1861, 18).

Victoria and Albert have imparted 'joys' and now 'griefs' to their subjects. Albert's death is the first sundering of 'the common lot' in an otherwise blissful reign. Rossetti's deployment of the cliché of the 'common lot' conveys a double edged image of death separating the living Victoria from the dead Albert and inextricably binding her individual grief with the 'common' grief of her subjects. Victoria's grief is not her own. The following three stanzas represent the layered grief of Victoria through the triune nature of her identity as Queen, wife and mother. Rossetti places the greatest emphasis on Victoria's role as 'the desolate Queen upon her throne'. She calls on God to 'strengthen her hands' and 'confirm her heart' so that she can 'bear a load alone/ Borne until now in part'. After stabilising Victoria's image as monarch, Rossetti represents her as 'the desolate woman in her home, / Broken of heart . . ./ Shrinking from solitary days to come, / Beggared tho' much is left'. From this image of isolated individual grief the poem expands into an appeal to Victoria's subjects as the 'Sons and Daughters' of a weeping mother. Rossetti calls on her readers to empathise with Victoria's grief and intermix their tears with their sovereign's, a demand which resembles Barrett's rhetorical blurring of Victoria and her subject's tears in *The Young Queen*. Rossetti consoles her readers and her Queen with the reminder that Albert 'only sleeps'. In the closing stanzas Rossetti cements the image of Victoria as a strong Queen who can rule alone and must be revered and loved with a 'double love'. However, there is an anxious undertone in these calls for absolute devotion; an anxiety reflecting the need to affirm political stability and national unity in England after Albert's removal from the familial tableaux which had functioned so effectively as an icon of social and national unity. Rossetti closes the poem with an expression of hope for Victoria's longevity and an image of eternal loyalty as the Queen, through death, is united once again with Albert: 'Then may her husband praise'.

Barrett's and Rossetti's poems dramatise the hybridity of the Victorian public sphere, in which private interests of family and morality assume public significance. Their representations of Victoria reflect a consciousness of the complex and contradictory nature of the public sphere in which a woman who is a queen must move. John Ruskin's lecture 'Of Queen's Gardens', published four years after the latest poem discussed in this chapter, exemplifies the symbolic valency of 'queenliness' in Victorian conceptions of private and public spheres. As Elisabeth Helsinger astutely observes, the newly critical role for women which Ruskin elucidates 'comes dangerously close to denying the true womanly ideal which inspired it' (1983, 1:79). Ruskin considers the idea of the 'royal authority' of women in the light of 'what special portion or kind of this royal authority, arising out of a noble education, may rightly be possessed by women; and how far they also are called to a true queenly power. Not in their household merely, but over all within their sphere.

And in what sense, if they rightly understood and exercised this royal gracious influence, the order and beauty induced by such benignant power would justify us in speaking of the territories over which each of them reigns as Queen's Gardens' (1865, 49-50) On one level this statement can be read as a manifesto for the separation of spheres, a reading which Walter Houghton extols in his celebratory description of Ruskin's lecture as 'the most important single document I know for the characteristic idealisation of love, woman, and the home in Victorian society' (1957, 343). Houghton's description of Ruskin's lecture as a quintessentially Victorian text fails to take into account the critical scepticism with which the lecture was met. Critics, at the time of its publication, condemned *Sesame and Lilies* as anachronistic and 'Carlylesque' (Helsinger, 1983, 1:79). By reading Ruskin's text as an articulation of separate sphere ideology Houghton fails to consider the blurring of 'home' and 'nation' inherent in the concept of women's power over their territory or garden. National order is inextricable from domestic stability, which women are 'called' to maintain: 'This is the true nature of home – it is the place of Peace; the shelter, not only from all injury, but from all terror, doubt, and division' (1865, 59). Ruskin rhetorically confuses public and private spheres in his desire to extend the role and influence of women and inadvertently reproduces the hybridity of the Victorian public sphere in which boundaries between feminine and masculine roles are perpetually in the process of negotiation. By playing with the boundaries between the domestic and the national Ruskin destabilises exactly what he tries to fix.

The metaphoric fluidity of queenliness entraps Ruskin even as it frees Victorian women poets to explore the public structuring of female sexuality in their culture. If we limit the possibilities of women identifying with Victoria to the constraints of domestic ideology and interpret the subjectivities it promulgates as an absolutist form, we remove women to an untenable site outside the language of authority and deprive them of agency in the direction of their gaze. There is no space for metaphorisation and scepticism in such a dichotomous model of identification. Women re-read formulaic stereotypes of masculinity and femininity rendering the closure such clichés encouraged as indeterminate and unstable. Victoria is the ultimate hybrid ideal, she is simultaneously public and private, professionally assertive and seemingly personally reticent. Victoria's public persona is always represented in terms of agency in women's poetry, whether it is her choice to assert her position in public life or enshroud herself in a spectacular display of grief after Albert's death. By simply representing Queen Victoria, women foregrounded gender within debates concerning national identity and the political agency of a woman as sovereign. The outcome of such a movement legitimises the role queenliness, as a political and moral characteristic of women, must play in the formulation of a coherent vision of England's duty to its empire.

References

Bhabha, H., 1990. *Nation and Narration*, London and New York: Routledge.
Barrett Browning, E. 1904. *Poetical Works*, London: Henry Frowde.
Benson, A.C. and Esher, Viscount., eds, 1907. *The Letters of Queen Victoria*, New York: Longmans.
Best, G. 1979. *Mid-Victorian Britain 1851–1875*, Glasgow: Fontana/Collins.
Cannadine, David. 1983. 'The Context, Performance and Meaning of Ritual: The British Monarchy and the 'Invention of Tradition', c. 1820–1977', *The Invention of Tradition*, eds. Hobsbawm, E. and Ranger, T. Cambridge: Cambridge University Press.
Cannadine, David. 1989. *Pleasures of the Past*, London: Collins.
Chorley, H. 1850. *Athenaeum*, June 1st, 585.
Colley, L. 1992. *Britons. Forging a Nation 1707–1837*, New Haven and London: Yale University Press.
Cooper, H. 1988. *Elizabeth Barrett Browning. Woman and Artist*, Chapel Hill and London: The University of North Carolina Press.
Crump, R., ed, 1979–90. *The Complete Poems of Christina Rossetti*, 3 vols, Baton Rouge and London: Louisiana State University Press.
Davidoff, L. and Hall, C. 1994. *Family Fortunes. Men and Women of the English Middle Class 1780–1850*, London: Routledge.
Ellis, S. 1843. *The Wives of England*, London.
———, 1846. *The Island Queen*, London.
Faithfull, E., ed. 1863. *Poems: An Offering to Lancashire. Printed and published for the Art Exhibition for the Relief of Distress in the Cotton Districts*, London.
'French Outrages in Tahiti'. August 1st, 1844. *The Times*, 3.
Fulford, R., ed, 1964. *Dearest Child: Letters between Queen Victoria and The Princess Royal, 1858–1861*, New York: Holt.
Gervais, D. 1993. *Literary Englands. Versions of Englishness in Modern Writing*, Cambridge and New York: Cambridge University Press.
Guedalla, P. 1934. *The Queen and Mr Gladstone*, New York: Doubleday.
Hardie, F. 1935. *The Political Influence of Queen Victoria*, London and Oxford: Oxford University Press.
Helsinger, E.K., Lauterbach Sheets, R. and Veeder, W., eds, 1983. *The Woman Question. Defining Voices, 1837–1883*, vol 1, New York and London: Garland.

Houghton, W. 1957. *The Victorian Frame of Mind, 1830–1870*, London: Yale University Press.
'Important Events in Tahiti'. August 3rd, 1844. *Illustrated London News*, 66.
Kaplan, C., ed, 1978. *Aurora Leigh* by Elizabeth Barrett Browning, London: The Women's Press.
Leighton, A. *Victorian Women Poets. Writing Against The Heart*, New York and London: Harvester Wheatsheaf.
Lucas, J. 1987/8. 'Love of England: the Victorians and Patriotism', *Browning Society Notes.*, 17, 63.
Miller, B., ed, 1959. *Elizabeth Barrett to Miss Mitford. The Unpublished Letters of Elizabeth Barrett Barrett to Mary Russell Mitford*, London: John Murray.
Norton, C. 1840. *The Dream and Other Poems*, London.
'Obituary for Albert, Prince Consort'. December 16, 1861. *The Times*, 8.
Pagden, A. 1993. *European encounters with the New World. From Renaissance to Romanticism*, New Haven and London: Harvard University Press.
Ricks, C. ed., 1969. *The Poems of Tennyson*, London and Harlow: Longmans.
Ruskin, J. 1866. *Sesame and Lilies*, London.
Sinfield, A. 1986. *Alfred Lord Tennyson*, Oxford: Basil Blackwell.
Strickland, A. 1840. *Queen Victoria. From Birth to Bridal*, London.
Woodham-Smith, C. 1972. *Queen Victoria. Her Life and Times 1819–1861*, London: Penguin.

The Politics of a Feminist Poetics: 'Armgart' and George Eliot's Critical Response to Aurora Leigh

LOUISE HUDD

> 'Within each woman the first, nameless love is singing'
> (Cixous and Clément 1986, 93)

WHISLT FEW WOULD now dispute the artistic and cultural significance of Elizabeth Barrett Browning's epic poem about female artistry, *Aurora Leigh* (1856), Bonnie J. Lisle's comment that 'One of the greatest English novelists, George Eliot remains at best a second-rate poet' (Lisle 1984, 263), is not entirely unjust. So why pay attention to George Eliot's verse drama 'Armgart' (1870)? Partly because, as a brief plot synopsis demonstrates, 'Armgart' exemplifies its author's notoriously edgy relationship with both nineteenth-century, and contemporary, feminism. The poem opens with the triumph of the opera singer Armgart in Gluck's *Orfeo ed Euridice* and her spirited rejection of a second marriage proposal from the diplomat Graf Dornberg, in which she resists his attempts to curtail her ambitions. The final three scenes are set a year after these events. Armgart has suffered a long illness and discovers that the 'strong remedies' used to save her life have destroyed the exquisite nature of her voice (Eliot 1870, 135). The poem ends with Armgart's renunciation of her operatic career to go to the provinces with her cousin Walpurga to teach music and singing.

The plot reads like an example of what Sandra Gilbert and Susan Gubar regard as George Eliot's 'feminine anti-feminism' (1979, 466), which many other critics have wrestled with since (see, for example: Beer 1986, 1–29, 147–199; David 1987, 177–196; and Nestor 1985, 141–166). The poem has become part of the contemporary debate about George Eliot's own status as a feminist, and it is probably due to this that 'Armgart' is read at all today. However, I shall argue that prompting discussion about the way in which women approach sexual politics was one of the aims of the poem in the first place and is part of its continuing importance. This essay regards 'Armgart' as a political critique of the idealistic feminism of Barrett Browning's

Aurora Leigh, and in particular, the earlier text's problematic depiction of class politics and social reform[1]. This response embraces George Eliot's criticism, letters, and *Scenes of Clerical Life*, as well as 'Armgart' itself. The background to this dialogue is the arena of Victorian sexual politics, since both poems contribute to the debate about the rights of women, the Woman Question.

Aurora Leigh was a significant contribution to the progress of Victorian feminism. Through the pseudo-autobiography of the poet Aurora Leigh it explored the problems of the woman writer. It tackled head on the conservative sexual ideology which was used to disenfranchise women, stressing that the work of the woman artist was both artistically and socially important. The poem's frank discussion of the sexual exploitation of women in British cities and of the rape of the seamstress Marian Erle has rightly been seen as a major part of its feminist challenge to the sexual double standards of its time. As Angela Leighton makes clear, the major importance of the poem was in its having been written at all: 'Barrett Browning's "feminist" purpose is rooted, not so much in her actual social message, as in her commitment to *write*, as a woman, against the odds of tradition and of continuing male prejudice' (1986, 8–9).

Aurora Leigh thus offered nineteenth-century women writers an inspiring model of ambitious female artistry, both in the career and vision of the poem's protagonist, and in the successfully realised ambition of Barrett Browning herself to write a female epic. One indication of its immediate impact is that less than six months after its first publication Elizabeth Gaskell used a quotation from Book V (ll. 434–441) as an epigraph to the first edition of her *The Life of Charlotte Brontë*, clearly directing the reader to a fictional model of artistic success by which to read Brontë's life. Barrett Browning and her poem were taken up by Victorian feminists and used as examples of female success and talent to support their assertion that women deserved greater access to education and work. Frances Power Cobbe's 'What shall we do with our old maids?', for example, praised the 'strength' of the poem, 'its sturdy wrestlings and grapplings . . . with all the sternest problems of our social life . . .

---

[1] Kathleen Blake has also noted the parallel between 'Armgart' and *Aurora Leigh*, but does not pursue it. She argues that: 'George Eliot confirms the representative ambivalence of the century's epic-scale portrait of the woman artist, Elizabeth Barrett Browning's *Aurora Leigh*' (Blake 1980, 75).

[which] takes us miles away from the received notion of a woman's poetry' (1862, 366).

George Eliot was also affected by the success of Elizabeth Barrett Browning's poetry, which she admired. George Eliot and George Henry Lewes read *Aurora Leigh* in November and December 1856, and again in June 1857. She commented in a letter to her friend Sara Hennell that 'Such books are among the great blessings of life' (Haight (ed.) 1954, 2, 282). George Eliot's longing to meet its author was finally fulfilled during her trip to Italy in the summer of 1860. Barrett Browning wrote to her sister-in-law Sarianna Browning in June 1860, telling her that: 'Mr. Lewes and Miss Evans have been here, and are coming back to settle into our congenial bosom. I admire her books so much, that certainly I shall not refuse to receive her' (Kenyon (ed.) 1897, 2, 400). More significantly, as well as reading the poem for pleasure, she reviewed *Aurora Leigh* in the 'Belles Lettres' section of the *Westminster Review* in January 1857.

George Eliot praised the poem, and recognised its importance to the development of the woman writer's claims to be taken seriously as an artist:

> Mrs. Browning is, perhaps, the first woman who has produced a work which exhibits all the peculiar powers without the negations of her sex; which superadds to masculine vigour, breadth, and culture, feminine subtlety of perception, feminine quickness of sensibility, and feminine tenderness. It is difficult to point to a woman of genius who is not either too little feminine, or too exclusively so. But in this, her longest and greatest poem, Mrs. Browning has shown herself all the greater poet because she is intensely a poetess. (1857a, 306)

The terms in which George Eliot praises Barrett Browning's achievement recall the justification for women's writing which lay behind her argument in 'Woman in France: Madame de Sablé' (1854), that because art and literature, 'imply the action of the entire being ... woman has something specific to contribute' (1854, 53). The review stresses that what distinguished *Aurora Leigh* was the very fact that it based its claims to be considered as a major work, not *despite* the fact that it was written by a woman, but *because* it was written by a woman. However, the manner in which the *Aurora Leigh* achieves this feminist success is at the root of George Eliot's critical and fictional response to the poem.

George Eliot's major criticism of the poem was its treatment of the social philanthropist Romney Leigh:

> The *story* of 'Aurora Leigh' has ... nothing either fresh or felicitous in structure or incident; and we are especially sorry that Mrs. Browning has added one more to the imitations of the catastrophe in 'Jane Eyre', by smiting her hero with blindness before he is made happy in the love of Aurora. Life has sadness and bitterness enough for a disappointed philanthropist like Romney Leigh, short of maiming or blindness... (1857a, 306)

She thus highlights something which concerned many critics at the time, the poem's attitude to social reform. John Nichol, in an article length review of *Aurora Leigh*, which also appeared in the *Westminster Review* in 1857, questioned what he considered to be the poem's political naiveté in its valorisation of the regime of Louis Napoleon, and its exaggeration of the socially reformative power of art:

> Art and the perfection of the poetic sentiments follow, or are contemporaneous with an age of prosperity. They do not constitute, nor can they supply the place of material comforts and free institutions. Artistic culture, far from standing in the place of philanthropic effort, depends upon the success of that effort for its own permanence. (Nichol 1857, 412)

The fact that Nichol's review of *Aurora Leigh* was written six months after George Eliot's 'Belles Lettres' assessment in the same journal, and that it also considered Romney Leigh's mutilation 'offensive' (1857, 411), perhaps indicates a degree of indebtedness to George Eliot's own thinking on the subject. Nichol's criticism is certainly reminiscent of the stance taken in George Eliot's own essays of the time, particularly 'The Natural History of German Life' (1856), with its emphasis upon realism in the representation of the life of the masses as part of the political task of increasing understanding between social groups:

> our social novels profess to represent the people as they are, and the unreality of their representations is a grave evil. The greatest benefit we owe to the artist, whether painter, poet, or novelist, is the extension of our sympathies. (1856, 270)

The one thing that *Aurora Leigh* isn't, is realist in the sense in which George Eliot conceives the term. Indeed, Barrett Browning's depiction of the poor bears out what Cora Kaplan has to say in her important introduction to The Women's Press edition of the poem: 'Nowhere in the literature of the mid-century is the bourgeois rejection of working-class consciousness more glaring than in *Aurora Leigh*' (1978, 35). Barrett Browning's emphasis upon the significance of the vision of the woman poet overdetermines everything else. Aurora encourages her fellow poets to:

> Never flinch,
> But still, unscrupulously epic, catch
> Upon the burning lava of a song
> The full-veined, heaving, double-breasted Age.
> (368, V, ll. 213–16)

Such a feminisation of the body politic is designed to reinforce the conclusion that the writer best suited to represent such an age is a woman poet. However, there is a sense of disjuncture in the poem between the body as a site which comes to represent a progression in sexual politics, and the use of the imagery of the body politic as the site of social struggle. The metaphors of the body politic are merged with the imagery of the female body, leaving the poem's critique of social conditions for the urban masses uneasily subordinated to its feminist message. Thus, it is the poor attending the class-uniting marriage of Romney Leigh and Marian Erle who are 'humours of the peccant social wound' and 'a dark slow stream, like blood' (332–3, IV, ll. 544, 554). Social division is thus represented, not so much as a rupture between classes, but as a fracture which is located in the threat of one class. The imagery of blood in the passage above, and later of milk (336, IV, l. 633), subsume the working classes into a wider nexus of metaphors derived from the female body which characterise the poem, in the same way that, as Kaplan suggests, a potentially radical critique of class is deflected into an implicit assertion of feminism: 'Inevitably a theory which identifies the radical practice of art with the achievement of radical social change, or asserts the unity of female experience without examining the forms taken by that experience in different social groups, will emerge with a theory of art and politics unconnected with material reality and deeply élitist' (1978, 12).

Barrett Browning always repudiated the charge that in blinding Romney Leigh she was imitating *Jane Eyre* (Kenyon (ed.) 1897, 2,

245-6). In a letter to Sarianna Browning she presented it as a symbol of the renovation of his views on gender and on the social role of female art:

> He had to be blinded, observe to be made to see; just as Marian had to be dragged through the uttermost debasement of circumstances to arrive at the sentiment of personal dignity.
>
> (Kenyon (ed.) 1897, 2, 242)

What is striking about Barrett Browning's language is that it emphasizes the absolute necessity of what the poem depicts, and that it specifically parallels Romney's fate with that of Marian Erle: both of them 'had to be' damaged. The fact that Barrett Browning links the fates of Romney and Marian so forcefully is fascinating. Indeed, the assailant who costs Romney his eyesight, thus bearing out the poem's view of the working classes as dangerous, ungrateful, and discordant, is Marian's father. Marian rejects Romney's offer of marriage and legitimacy for the child born from her rape to state that she has

> come to learn – a woman, poor or rich,
> Despised or honoured, is a human soul,
> And what her soul is, that she is herself.
>
> (565, IX, 328–330)

Of course, she has come to learn this from Aurora herself, exchanging Romney's ideology for a new one. Although her words strike a blow for female independence from male standards of sexual conduct, they are also convenient for the plot, leaving Romney and Aurora free to marry. Indeed, it is in this renunciation, as much as in her reactions to her rape, that Marian Erle becomes the type of 'heroic artisan' which 'The Natural History of German Life' had condemned as a 'misrepresentation' of the lot of the people (Eliot 1856, 271).

The only person in the poem who isn't physically injured or degraded is Aurora herself. Romney himself believes that in losing his sight he has been 'Turned out of nature, mulcted as a man' (574, IX, l. 564). To mulct is both to deprive and to punish. If Romney is being punished it is presumably for his failure to take Aurora's art seriously, and his wrong-headed subordination of love to social reform. However, the word 'mulct' was used once before, but of Aurora herself, in Lady Waldemar's description of the poet's superiority to the rest of her sex:

> You stand outside,
> You artist women, of the common sex;
> You share not with us, and exceed us so
> Perhaps by what you're mulcted in, your hearts
> Being starved to make your heads...
> (277, III, ll. 406–410)

Lady Waldemar's belief that the female artist is separated from her sex because she lacks a heart is triumphantly reversed by the poem. Aurora testifies subsequently that she has found her true womanliness in her love for Romney, but as she also reminds us: 'No perfect artist is developed here/ From any imperfect woman' (577, IX, ll. 648–9). She has not relinquished her art, and does not perceive it as being in opposition to her femininity; rather, to accept Romney's love and thus, in her own terms, confirm her womanhood, is to make her a perfect woman and hence a perfect artist.

The costs involved in achieving this artistic perfection are addressed in 'Armgart'. It restages the themes of *Aurora Leigh*, continuing Barrett Browning's disquisition upon the place of the female artist in Victorian society. It explores the obligations of the exceptional woman to her society and to other women, raising the issue of what it means to be marginalised in the interests of a political action which might liberate only the exceptional few rather than the many. 'Armgart' questions the idealised solution to the troubling social problems which Barrett Browning broaches in the early books of the poem and the political implications of having a single narrative voice express a revolutionary social ideology which will develop 'new societies' (587, IX, l. 948).

Before I go on to analyse 'Armgart' I want to look at what I believe to be George Eliot's initial fictional response to *Aurora Leigh*, 'Mr Gilfil's Love-Story', from her first published work *Scenes of Clerical Life* (1857). The date of the composition of this fiction is important. George Eliot began writing the story on Christmas Day 1856, sending the first six chapters to John Blackwood on 11 February 1857 and dispatching the final parts in April. It was printed in four instalments in *Blackwood's Edinburgh Magazine* between March and June. The composition of this scene of clerical life therefore coincided with George Eliot's re-reading of *Aurora Leigh* and the writing of her review of the poem for the *Westminster Review*. Indeed, in the letter to William Blackwood in which she writes herself George Eliot for the first time, she apologises for being 'behind-hand' on the story as the result of 'other business', part of which must have included the 'Belles Lettres' section which had appeared in January (Haight (ed.) 1954, 2, 292). Furthermore, the name of its female protagonist Caterina Sarti perhaps recalls Barrett Browning's 'Catarina to Camoens' (1832), which had been inspired by the love story of the sixteenth century Portuguese poet Luís Vaz de Camões and Catherina de Ataide. The narrator is Camoens' dying muse and the poem's themes of abandonment by a faithless lover, a decline into early death, and the voicing of the female response to male objectification, are also significant in 'Mr Gilfil's Love-Story'.

As in *Aurora Leigh* Italy and England are contrasted as lands of repression and passion respectively. Like Aurora, Caterina Sarti is transplanted from her native Italy, following her musician father's death, to be brought up in England by Sir Christopher and Lady Cheverel. Lady Henrietta's orthodox views on feminine behaviour would strike a chord with Aurora's Aunt Leigh. Caterina, like Aurora, struggles against that repression of her emotions which is expected of her in the genteel world to which she has been removed. Unlike Aurora, however, she is always kept on the margins of English society, perpetually foreign. She is, for instance, never adopted by Sir Christopher and Lady Cheverel and physical descriptions of her emphasize her darkness and her ardent nature, which are seen as Italian attributes. The only means by which she can successfully express the emotions she feels is through music:

> Her singing was what she could do best; it was her one point of superiority . . . her love, her jealousy, her pride, her rebellion against her destiny, made one stream of passion which welled forth in the deep rich tones of her voice. (Eliot 1857b, c.2, 96)

Although Caterina's rebellion is, in this instance, against a specific destiny, Anthony Wybrow's courtship of Miss Assher, it is also linked to wider movements in the world beyond Cheverel Manor.

Caterina is singing in the summer of 1788 and her disturbed state is equated by the narrator with that of pre-Revolutionary France:

> In that summer, we know, the great nation of France was agitated

> by conflicting thoughts and passions, which were but the beginning of sorrows. And in our Caterina's little breast, too, there were terrible struggles. The poor bird was beginning to flutter and vainly dash its soft breast against the iron bars of the inevitable . . . (c.3, 99–100)

The overstrained image of Caterina as a caged bird recalls the position of Aurora Leigh in her aunt's house as 'A wild bird scarcely fledged . . . brought to her cage', and expected to live, like her aunt, 'A sort of cage-bird life' (175–6, I, l. 310; l. 305). These lines relating to the confinement of women in the conventions of accepted sexual ideology obviously struck George Eliot, since they are quoted in one of the extracts from the poem offered in 'Belles Lettres' (1857a, 308).[2] In conjunction with the reference to France, however, they widen the consequences of the repression of feminine self-expression into a specifically political issue for the nation, as well as a personal curtailment of freedom. When Maynard Gilfil tells Caterina that she must control her emotions his advice is couched in a rhetoric already sliding into the political: 'the peace of the whole family depends on your power of governing yourself' (c.9, 137). Caterina's self-control within the family is thus equated with the peace of the nation of which the family forms a fundamental unit. These are the arguments of the England of the 1850s as much as the 1780s and 90s. It was believed that if women forgot the importance of their morally exemplary role as wives and mothers, then society would be riven.[3] Furthermore, contemporary feminists were keen to make the link between the state of the nation and the condition of the women in it. In the same volume of the *Westminster Review* which contains George Eliot's review of *Aurora Leigh*, there was an article by Caroline Frances Cornwallis on the 'Capabilities and Disabilities of Women'; it ominously compared England to Athens, remarking that if women were not educated to use their talents, the nation would fall to barbarism as did the earlier civilisation, which had also scorned the place of its female inhabitants (1857, 71–2).

---

[2] The extract is entitled 'A Portrait' and comprises lines 270–309 of Book One.
[3] For more on the ideology of female domesticity in the nineteenth century see: Nancy Armstrong, *Desire and Domestic Fiction: A Political History of the Novel* (New York and Oxford, 1987); Anita Levy, *Other Women: The Writing of Class, Race, and Gender, 1832–1898* (Princeton, N.J., 1991); Mary Poovey, *Uneven Developments: The Ideological Work of Gender in Mid-Victorian England* (1988; London, 1989).

Although 'Mr Gilfil's Love-Story' raises the revolutionary potential of women, it avoids a direct confrontation with the issue; Anthony dies as a result of a heart attack rather than the murder which Caterina had planned, whilst his would-be assassin is safely married to Gilfil and goes into a fatal decline. Sir Christopher still gets the outcome he desired, the marriage of Gilfil and Caterina, but he is forced to reconsider the costs to others of his 'inflexible will'. Like Romney Leigh he comes to question the certainty of his vision: 'I thought I saw everything, and was stone-blind all the while' (c.18, 170). Even music itself is redefined as part of Caterina's redemption from unhealthy passion: 'The soul that was born anew to music was born anew to love' (c.20, 183). 'Mr Gilfil's Love-Story' thus broaches the subject of female discontent only to contain it, but the relationship between domesticity, revolution, and singing is readdressed in the later poem.

One of the pieces through which Caterina expresses her passion and rebellion is the aria 'Che farò senza Euridice?' from act III of Christoph Gluck's *Orfeo ed Euridice*. It is the same opera in which Armgart has her triumph. *Orfeo ed Euridice* (1762) was one of the standard works of the nineteenth century repertory and George Eliot saw it performed in Berlin on 2 January 1855. Although the role of Orfeo had originally been created for the castrato Guadagni, in the nineteenth century it was customary for the role to be sung by a woman. In 1859, for example, Berlioz had adapted the role for the contralto Pauline Viardot-Garcia.[4] The performance of the opera which George Eliot saw in Berlin had as Orfeo the niece of Richard Wagner, Johanna Jachmann Wagner. Indeed, George Eliot commented in a letter to Sara Hennell that: 'The voices – except in the choruses – are all women's voices' (Haight (ed.) 1954, 2, 191). On the day that George Eliot relayed her reactions to *Orfeo* to her friend Sara Hennell she had attended another opera in which a woman spends much of her time on stage pretending to be a man, Beethoven's *Fidelio* (Haight (ed.) 1954, 2, 191, n.4). Gillian Beer has argued that it was the fact that the role of Orfeo was sung by a woman which gave the opera its importance to George Eliot:

---

[4] An article entitled 'Music about Music' in *All the Year Round* 17 (1867) 256–259, declared that Orpheus had found 'a perfect exponent' in Madame Viardot (257). For more on the opera see Patricia Howard (ed.), *C.W. von Gluck: Orfeo* (Cambridge, 1981), esp. the essay by Eve Barsham, 'The Opera in the Nineteenth Century', 84–98.

The figure of the woman singer dressed as a man, releasing the loved woman Eurydice from death by the value of her music, had a particular value for George Eliot: she too was known as a woman artist, though clad in a man's name. (1986, 211–12)

Performance as a man forms part of the discourse of sexual politics which characterises both 'Armgart' and *Aurora Leigh*. The imagery of the woman being clad as a man is used by Aurora Leigh to describe her attempts to absorb the contents of her father's library: 'He wrapped his little daughter in his large/ Man's doublet, careless did it fit or no.' (192, I, ll. 727–8). These lines are inverted by Armgart after the loss of the voice when she fears that she will be:

> Prisoned in all the petty mimicries
> Called woman's knowledge, that will fit the world
> As doll-clothes fit a man. (144)

Both reactions reveal a sense of dissonance between a valorised and desired knowledge which is the prerogative of men, and the lives of women who seek that knowledge. There is a further irony in the sense in which Armgart's words evoke the mimicries in which she has been engaged in her performance. She denigrates the specifically feminine, incapable of doing what George Eliot believed that Barrett Browning had done with *Aurora Leigh*, and truly expressing her sex through her art. This reminds us of what George Eliot had to say in 'Woman in France' about most books written by women: 'when not a feeble imitation, they are usually an absurd exaggeration of the masculine style, like the swaggering gait of a bad actress in male attire' (1854, 53). The woman attempting to penetrate the world of masculine knowledge and power risks being seen as no more than a principal boy. The female performer can only act as a man, but she will be judged as a woman. As Armgart is aware, the audience during her performance at first evaluate not her artistry, but 'the price/Of such a woman in the social mart' (120).

In performing on stage Armgart risks the sort of reaction provoked by the actress Vashti in Charlotte Brontë's *Villette*, whom John Graham Bretton 'judged ... as a woman, not an artist: it was a branding judgment' (Brontë 1853, c.23, 373). Vashti was based upon the French tragedian Eliza Rachel Felix, known simply to her Victorian audience as Rachel, and it has been suggested that Armgart's character is derived partly from Brontë's portrait and from what George Eliot knew of Rachel herself (Barrett 1989, 175–6).[5] George Eliot had read *Villette* and made the connection between the French actress and Brontë's character when she saw Rachel perform in London in 1853, and was disappointed that she had 'not yet seen the "Vashti" of Currer Bell' (*Letters* 2, 104). More important than any specific attribution however, is the fact that Armgart, like Vashti/Rachel, is a performer. The artistry of these women is derived from the body itself, and their performances thus stage in very direct terms the conflict between the perception of sex and the social interpretation of it in gender.

As a singer Armgart faces the same conflict between her art and what is expected of her as a woman that was experienced by any female artist. Gillian Beer has asserted that George Eliot's 'chosen figure for the creative woman is not the writer . . . it is the musician, and in particular the singer' (1986, 202) and the figure of the singer, has a particular resonance for George Eliot as a *poet*.[6] Poetry was often equated with song. In George Eliot's review she had regarded *Aurora Leigh* as the Caterina Sarti-like expression of 'a full mind pouring itself out in song as its natural and easiest medium' (1857a, 307). Whilst the year before 'Armgart' was written George Eliot had asserted that although music and poetry could not be fully paralleled, 'in their fundamental principles' they were 'analogous' (1869, 287). The criticism of the two was also analogous. The reactions to Armgart's singing reflect the sort of criticism which *Aurora Leigh* was written to challenge, but which it nonetheless provoked. Although a review in the *Dublin University Magazine* could comment that 'Aurora is Elizabeth' (1862, 158), it nonetheless concluded of Barrett Browning that:

> Her faults were of her womanhood: her great achievements were her own . . . But the blemishes which we see in her works . . . may

[5] For the impact of Rachel on her contemporaries see also George Henry Lewes, 'Rachel', *On Actors and the Art of Acting* (London, 1875), pp. 23–31 and John Stokes, 'Rachel's "Terrible Beauty": An Actress Among the Novelists', *ELH* 51 (1984) 771–793.

[6] The significance of the voice and of the figure of the singer in George Eliot's work is discussed in Beer 1986, 200–213. As will become clear, this essay is indebted to her sensitive reading of the issue. The complex and important relationship between George Eliot's fiction and music is explored in Delia da Sousa Correa's 'George Eliot and Music in Nineteenth-Century Literature' (D.Phil. thesis, Oxford, 1993) and Beryl Gray, *George Eliot and Music* (Basingstoke, 1989).

teach woman especially, a weighty lesson. The function of woman is – not to write, not to act, not to be famous – but to love.

(1862, 162)

It is the sort of argument used by the Graf to persuade Armgart to marry him:

> Pain had been saved,
> Nay, purer glory reached, had you been throned
> As woman only, holding all your art
> As attribute to that dear sovereignty. (129)

Armgart rejects both the Graf's reasoning, and his proposal, asserting that: 'I am an artist by my birth – /By the same warrant that I am a woman' (129). Like Aurora Leigh, she refuses to acknowledge that there is a conflict between her sex, the expectations of her sex, and her art. She argues against the 'oft-taught Gospel' that motherhood is the best and most natural expression of femininity, seeing her voice *and* her ambition as being as natural as motherhood, both equally the gifts of Nature (128). Like a Victorian feminist she regards the natural as a theoretical position which can be challenged like any other: 'I need not crush myself within a mould/ Of theory called Nature' (129–30). The concept of 'a natural sex' was as troubling to many Victorian feminists as it is to modern theorists like Judith Butler (1990). In *The Subjection of Women* (written 1861, published 1869) John Stuart Mill questioned the legitimacy of justifying female inferiority through an appeal to biological weakness, and stressed that the whole issue of what is natural to each sex was profoundly mistaken: 'What is now called the nature of women is an eminently artificial thing – the result of forced repression in some directions, unnatural stimulation in others' (1869, 493).

'Armgart' locates the question of the natural not just within the discourse of sexual politics, but also within national politics. In this, the poem fleshes out an idea expressed fifteen years earlier in a letter George Eliot sent to John Chapman from Berlin shortly after having seen *Orfeo*. She had suggested that she would like to write articles on the 'Ideals of Womankind', and on 'Woman in Germany', which was to explore 'woman as she presents herself to us in all the phases of development through which the German race has run' (Haight (ed.) 1954, 2, 190). Presumably, this article would have been modelled on 'Woman in France'. As in 'Mr Gilfil's Love-Story', the language which is used to characterise Armgart's singing is imbued with a sense of the political implications of female behaviour.

Armgart's mentor Leo calls her 'the queen of song!' (117). But Graf Dornberg, sounding like the reviewer of Barrett Browning for the *Dublin University Magazine*, asserts that:

> A woman's rank
> Lies in the fullness of her womanhood:
> Therein alone she is royal. (128)

The Graf redefines any pretension to political power or to the type of autonomy and ambition to excel which characterise Armgart's view of her art purely in terms of excellence in conformity to the demands of a natural sex. His use of the language of national politics brings to mind George Eliot's intentions in 'Woman in Germany' to consider the role of women in the development of the German race. The Graf's argument echoes that frequently made by the opponents of the extension of public work and rights to women. In Margaret Oliphant's response to Barbara Leigh Smith Bodichon's important appeal for a reform of the property laws relating to women, *A Brief Summary, in Plain Language, of the Most Important Laws Concerning Women* (1854), she commented that because a wife could 'Rule the house' she was 'a lawmaker, supreme and absolute; and yet, most despotic and unconstitutional of monarchs, you hear them weeping over infringed rights and powers denied' (1856, 387). Even most Victorian feminists themselves supported the Victorian ideology of home. Bessie Rayner Parkes, for example, writing in *The English Woman's Journal*, whilst desirous that single woman could obtain suitable employment, nonetheless argued that:

> The wife, in our civilisation, is the centre of domestic but also of social life ... were it otherwise the whole constitution of modern society would literally go to pieces. (1862, 204–5)

Women were thus seen as the key to national stability.

This gives a new force to the Graf's fear that Armgart harbours 'Caesar's ambition in her delicate breast' (116). The allusion to Caesar emphasizes the potential threat that the ambitious woman poses to the status quo. Caesar, after all, was responsible for the destruction of the Roman Republic and the restoration of monarchic rule. Furthermore, it invokes the national consequences of the revolutionary potential of the woman who bucked the system which 'Mr Gilfil's Love-Story' had raised and then evaded. This is perhaps made more explicit in what is said of the nature of the voice which is the focus of Armgart's identity as an artist, and thus of her resistance to the accepted social order. Walpurga tells the Graf that Armgart believes that 'Without that voice for channel to her soul', she would have become 'a Maenad' (117). Her singing thus helps to regulate the female excess associated with the maenad, the follower of Dionysus, who was associated with exclusively female rites, sexual expression, and violence, especially directed against men. The image of the maenad was also used to characterise the female sans-culottes of the French Revolution. The chapter which deals with the Insurrection of Women (October 1789) in Thomas Carlyle's *The French Revolution*, for example, is entitled 'The Menads' (1837, I, 260–64). So, like Caterina Sarti, Armgart's voice, as the expression of her anger and discontent at being a woman, has a revolutionary potential. The desire for rebellion is reinforced in Armgart's reaction to the loss of her career:

> ... Heaven made me royal – wrought me out
> With subtle finish towards pre-eminence,
> Made every channel of my soul converge
> To one high function, and then flung me down
> ...
> An inborn passion gives a rebel's right:
> I would rebel and die in twenty worlds
> Sooner than bear the yoke of thwarted life.   (144–45)

As Gilbert and Gubar are right to point out, Armgart models herself upon that arch rebel, Satan (1979, 454). The lines also recall Lucy Snowe's view of Vashti's performance as one in which 'each maenad movement [is] royally, imperially, incedingly upborne' and where 'Fallen, insurgent, banished, she remembers the heaven where she rebelled' (Brontë 1853, c.23, 370).

However, the poem does not allow Armgart's conception of herself as a female Lucifer to go unchallenged. It is her cousin and companion Walpurga who attacks Armgart's view of herself as a Miltonic rebel:

> Where is the rebel's right for you alone?
> Noble rebellion lifts a common load;
> But what is he who flings his own load off
> And leaves his fellows toiling? Rebel's right?
> Say rather, the deserter's. (146)

Walpurga's comments reveal the inherent contradiction in Armgart's rhetoric of rebellion, its use of monarchic imagery; it expresses a desire for the freedom of the one rather then the many and is fundamentally hierarchic and anti-democratic. All of Armgart's arguments against the Graf's patriarchal sexual ideology were valid, but they were based upon her being an exception to other women, upon her individualism, rather than a defence of the rights of all women to enjoy her liberty of action. In her wish for rebellion she shares the discourse of monarchic rule which characterised her exchanges with the Graf. She thus represented her voice as the guarantee of her separation from the rest of her sex:

> ... my song
> Was consecration, lifted me apart
> From the crowd chiselled like me, sister forms,
> But empty of divineness. (140)

It is interesting that the opera which she cannot sing is *Fidelio*. It could be argued that her failure to sing the role is precisely due to the fact that she has rejected the wifely devotion represented by Leonore, when she spurned the Graf. However, *Fidelio* is not just a paean to married love. Florestan is a political prisoner imprisoned for a love of liberty. The male disguise which Leonore adopts is a strategy to release her husband, just as Orpheus seeks to release Eurydice from Hades. What matters in both operas is liberation. As Armgart mourns the liberty she feels she has lost with her voice, Walpurga bursts out: 'Your wish has been a bolt to keep me in.' (144) Armgart's conception of revolution may emphasize liberty, but is alien to equality and fraternity. The poem is not condemning revolutionary action, but questioning the intellectual basis of Armgart's espousal of such a Romantic ideal. Her desire to be a rebel dramatizes the self, rhetorically maintaining her individuality even as she faces '"The Woman's Lot: a Tale of Everyday"' (Eliot 1870, 143). Indeed, rather than threatening the patriarchal status quo she confirms its fundamental function by stressing that even in revolt she is an exception to the female norm.

Most criticism of the poem has rightly tended to focus upon it as a dramatization of George Eliot's discomfort with the egoism of artistic ambition which she herself experienced (Lisle 1984; Newton 1973; Bodenheimer 1990; 1994, 161–188). Rosemarie Bodenheimer demonstrates how George Eliot employed her own position as an exceptional woman to evade requests for a more active involvement in feminist politics, keeping to the sidelines of the debate being more vigorously pursued by feminist friends like Barbara Bodichon (1994, 176–178). However, as Walpurga's intervention demonstrates, the poem was not just a personal psychomachia; its discourse of revolution reveals that egoism has serious political, not just moral, consequences.

A major element of this political critique is that the attack on Armgart's egoism is not just associated with the Graf, but with her cousin Walpurga. Rosemarie Bodenheimer regards what Walpurga has to say as 'the female obverse of the patriarchal ideology ... [Armgart] rejected in the Graf', and approvingly argues that Armgart 'translates Walpurga's ideas into sympathy and identification not with other women but with her fellow artist', Leo (1994, 182). Even Gillian Beer seems to imply that as a 'songless, ordinary woman' (Beer 1986, 212) Walpurga does not understand the difficulties of the artist. This is, I think, to replicate Armgart's marginalisation of the 'ordinary woman' and to valorise the exemption of the artist from a collective struggle which is one of the major concerns of the poem. I would argue that in locating the radical political critique of the poem in the mouth of the ordinary woman 'Armgart' attacks such a subordination of the marginal figure who becomes either the servant or the silent object of the ideals of the artistic woman. In doing so, the poem adds something to Aurora Leigh's presentation of Marian Erle.

Although Armgart's treatment of Walpurga cannot be compared with Aurora's of Marian, since Aurora has tried to bring the plight of her fellow women to the attention of society through her poetry, whilst Armgart has treated Walpurga 'As cushioned nobles use a weary serf' (146), the question of the objectification of the ordinary woman is an issue in both poems. Angela Leighton considers Marian Erle to be the index of 'Barrett Browning's new poetics ... of a woman conscious of her imagination's responsibility towards her sex', seeing Marian as 'the muse of this "unscrupulously epic" poem' (1986, 154; 156). However, to be a muse is to be robbed of subjectivity, to be set apart and seen as an icon: 'I'll find a niche/ And set thee there, my saint' (462, VII, ll. 126–7). George Eliot restores subjectivity and importance to the ordinary woman, and in doing so broadens the base of Barrett Browning's feminist aims.

In *Aurora Leigh* there is only one controlling narrative voice, Aurora's. Although other voices speak within the text they are always, by the very nature of the first person narrative which is used, refracted through Aurora's sensibility. Thus, on hearing Marian's story, Aurora 'writ/ The thing I understood so, than the thing/ I heard so' (318, IV, ll. 154–56). The very poetic form of *Aurora Leigh* subordinates the suffering myriads into the story of the struggle of the one. Indeed, the poem constructs this very division between individual and collective assertion as a sexed opposition: 'the love of all/ (To risk in turn a woman's paradox)/ Is but a small thing to the love of one' (378, V, ll. 479–81). However, 'Armgart' is a verse drama, which, like the libretto of an opera, is inherently polyphonous. It refuses the domination of the single voice. Armgart has emphasized the importance of her voice to the neglect of the very quality upon which it relies for its effect, listening, whereas Walpurga has had to 'listen, always listen' (145). Roland Barthes commented that 'The voice, in relation to silence, is like writing . . . on blank paper'; it is through listening that 'the voice inaugurates the relation to the Other' (1986, 255). The poetic form chosen by George Eliot offers the sort of interdependent unity which forms the basis of a political ideology which stresses that the collective need outweighs the ambition of the individual, and that social forms themselves are part of 'the grander evolution of things' (Eliot 1856, 299).

There is another formal difference between 'Armgart' and *Aurora Leigh*. One is 'unscrupulously epic', the other, at least in its first published form in *Macmillan's Magazine*, appeared with a subtitle as 'Armgart: A Tragic Poem' (Eliot 1871). Perhaps there is an element of wishing to surpass the earlier poem since Aristotle had argued in the *Poetics* that tragedy was a superior art form to the epic (Aristotle 1960, 116). However, it is more likely that the decision to write tragedy rather than epic was part of the political questioning I have discussed earlier. George Eliot's chief objection to Gluck's version of the Orpheus myth was its happy ending: 'But the worst of it is, that instead of letting it be a tragedy, Euridice is brought to life again' (Haight (ed.) 1954, 2, 191). In the subtitle to the poem George Eliot thus restored the tragic dimension of the Orpheus myth which was elided in Gluck's version, reminding the reader of the Virgilian and Ovidian versions of the story. Orpheus the supreme poet turned his back on women following the loss of Eurydice and was ripped to pieces in consequence by maenads angry at his rejection. When Leo says that 'Orpheus was Armgart, Armgart Orpheus' (121) the political purpose of the subtitle becomes clearer. The supreme artist cannot afford to exercise art at the cost of neglecting communal obligations, especially if that artist is a woman. *Aurora Leigh* ends with a revelatory vision of the New Jerusalem she and Romney are to try and build: 'The first foundations of that new, near Day/Which should be builded out of Heaven to God' (587, IX, 956–7). In a note upon the historical imagination George Eliot commented:

> Utopian pictures help the reception of ideas as to constructive results, but hardly so much as a vivid presentation of how results have been actually brought about, especially in religious and social change. And there is the pathos, the heroism often accompanying the decay and final struggles of old systems, which has not had its share of tragic commemoration. (Pinney 1963, 446–7, 447)

Aurora Leigh could offer only vision, not results, and it is through 'Armgart' perhaps that George Eliot offers a 'tragic commemoration' of a political and sexual system which, though being challenged, was still claiming victims.

It is appropriate that a poem which places so much emphasis upon the voice, and upon the need to listen, should itself form part of a critical dialogue with another text. 'Armgart' represents in the career of its heroine the ambition and inspirational vision of the female artist represented by both Aurora and Barrett Browning, whilst questioning the political costs involved in the pursuit of that feminist ideal, the attack upon the type of practical social reform desired by Romney Leigh, and the objectification of other women. In this it can be seen to restate both the praise and the concerns of the 'Belles Lettres' review. The relationship with *Aurora Leigh* did not cease with 'Armgart'. In 1874 George Eliot returned to 'Armgart' to prepare it for publication in *The Legend of Jubal* (1874). The subtitle which had been used in *Macmillan's* was dropped. Perhaps following the publication of *Middlemarch* Armgart's renunciation of her career could no longer be seen as a tragedy. Dorothea Brooke can find 'no epic life' like that of Aurora but this is attributed to the 'imperfect social state' in which she lives, implying that the growing freedom of women is a gradual historical process dependent upon the practicality of 'unhistoric acts' (Eliot 1871–2, 3; 824; 825), the sort of localised action which Armgart provides through her teaching in Freiburg. The conflict between individual and collective action which 'Armgart' exposed in *Aurora Leigh* is revisited in *Daniel Deronda*. The opera singer Alchirisi turns her back upon her race to pursue her ambitions as a female artist, whilst Mirah Cohen rejects her singing career to literally found a new Jerusalem, a new Jewish state, with Daniel Deronda, in a final chapter which has echoes of the conclusion to Barrett Browning's poem. 'Armgart' thus marks an important stage in the evolution of George Eliot's literary relationship with *Aurora Leigh*. It proves that although she may be a 'second-rate poet', she remains a first rate assessor of the political implications involved in the necessary process of developing a socially effective feminist poetics.

I would like to thank Kate Flint for her insightful and helpful criticism of earlier drafts of this essay, and Vincent Quinn for his comments and support.

References

All the Year Round 17 [author unknown] 1867. 'Music About Music', 256–259.
Aristotle 1960. *The Poetics*, in *Aristotle The Poetics, 'Longinus', On the Sublime, Demetrius, On Style*, London: William Heinemann, and Cambridge, Mass.: Harvard University Press. The Loeb edition, first published 1927.
Barrett, Dorothea 1989. *Vocation and Desire: George Eliot's Heroines*, London and New York: Routledge.
Barthes, Roland 1986. *The Responsibility of Forms: Critical Essays on Music, Art, and Representation*, trans. Richard Howard, Oxford: Basil Blackwell. Originally published as *L'obvie et l'obtus*, Paris: Éditions du Seuil, 1982.
Beer, Gillian 1986. *George Eliot*, Brighton: Harvester Press.
Blake, Kathleen 1980. 'Armgart – George Eliot on the Woman Artist', *Victorian Poetry*, 18, 75–80.
Bodenheimer, Rosemarie 1990. 'Ambition and Its Audiences: George Eliot's Performing Figures', *Victorian Studies*, 34, 7–33.
———, 1994. *The Real Life of Mary Ann Evans: George Eliot, Her Letters and Fiction*, Ithaca and London: Cornell University Press, 1994.
Brontë, Charlotte 1853. *Villette*, eds. Herbert Rosengarten and Margaret Smith, Oxford: Clarendon Press.
Browne, Matthew [W.B. Rands] 1868. 'George Eliot as a Poet', *Contemporary Review*, 8, 387–396.

Browning, Elizabeth Barrett 1856. *Aurora Leigh*, ed. Margaret Reynolds, Athens: Ohio University Press, 1992.
Butler, Judith 1990. *Gender Trouble: Feminism and the Subversion of Identity*, New York and London: Routledge.
Carlyle, Thomas 1837. *The French Revolution: A History*, eds. K.J. Fielding and David Sorensen, Oxford: Oxford University Press, 1989. The text is based on that of the 1857 edition.
Cixous, Hélène and Clément, Catherine 1986. *The Newly Born Woman*, trans. Betsy Wing, Manchester: Manchester University Press. First published in French as *La Jeune Née*, Paris: Union Générale d'Éditions, 1975.
Cobbe, Frances Power 1862. 'What shall we do with our old maids?', reprinted in Lacey 1987, 354–377. First published *Fraser's Magazine*, 66, 594–610.
[Cornwallis, Caroline Frances] 1857. 'Capabilities and Disabilities of Women', *Westminster Review* N.S. 11; O.S. 67, 42–72.
David, Deirdre 1987. *Intellectual Women and Victorian Patriarchy: Harriet Martineau, Elizabeth Barrett Browning, George Eliot*, Basingstoke: Macmillan.
Dublin University Magazine 60, [Author Unknown], 1862. 'Elizabeth Barrett Browning', 157–162.
Eliot, George 1854. 'Woman in France: Madame de Sablé', reprinted in Pinney 1963, 52–81. The article originally appeared in the *Westminster Review*, 62, 448–73.
———, 1856. 'The Natural History of German Life', in Pinney 1963, 266–299. First published in the *Westminster Review*, 66, 51–79.
———, 1857a. 'Belles Lettres', *Westminster Review*, n.s. 11; O.S. 67, 306–326.
———, 1857b. 'Mr Gilfil's Love-Story', *Scenes of Clerical Life*, ed. Thomas A. Noble, Oxford: Clarendon Press, 1985.
———, 1869. 'Versification', in *A Writer's Notebook 1854–1879 and Uncollected Writings*, ed. Joseph Wiesenfarth, Charlottesville: University Press of Virginia, 1981, 286–290.
———, 1870. 'Armgart', in *Collected Poems*, ed. Lucien Jenkins, London: Skoob, 1989.
———, 1871. 'Armgart', *Macmillan's Magazine*, 24, 161–187.
———, 1871–2. *Middlemarch*, ed. David Carroll, Oxford: Clarendon Press, 1986).
Gilbert, Sandra M. and Gubar, Susan 1979. *The Madwoman in the Attic: The Woman Writer and the Nineteenth-Century Literary Imagination*, New Haven and London: Yale University Press, 1984.
Haight, Gordon S. (ed.). *The George Eliot Letters*, 9 Vols., London: Oxford University Press and New Haven: Yale University Press, 1954–1978.
Kenyon, Frederic (ed.) 1897. *The Letters of Elizabeth Barrett Browning*, 2 Vols., London: Smith, Elder.
Lacey, Candida Ann, ed., 1987. *Barbara Leigh Smith Bodichon and the Langham Place Group*, New York and London: Routledge & Kegan Paul.
Lisle, Bonnie J. 1984. 'Art and Egoism in George Eliot's Poetry', *Victorian Poetry*, 22, 263–278.
Mill, John Stuart 1869. *The Subjection of Women*, reprinted in *On Liberty and Other Essays*, ed. John Gray, Oxford: Oxford University Press, 1991.
Nestor, Pauline 1985. *Female Friendships and Communities: Charlotte Brontë, George Eliot, Elizabeth Gaskell*, Oxford: Clarendon Press.

Newton, K.M. 1973. 'Byronic Egoism and George Eliot's *The Spanish Gypsy*', *Neophilologus*, 57, 388–400.
[Nichol, John] 1857. 'Aurora Leigh', *Westminster Review*, N.S. 12; O.S. 68, 399–415.
[Oliphant, Margaret] 1856. 'The Laws Concerning Women', *Blackwood's Edinburgh Magazine*, 79, 379–387.
Parkes, Bessie Rayner 1862. 'The Balance of Public Opinion in Regard to Woman's Work', in Lacey 1987, 200–205. Reprinted from *The English Woman's Journal* (July 1862).
Pinney, Thomas, ed., 1963. *Essays of George Eliot*, London: Routledge and Kegan Paul.

Poetry and Politics in the 1920s
JOHN LUCAS

THERE IS A widely-accepted view that in the aftermath of the Great War and faced with what seemed to be a wrecked Europe, poets saw themselves as required to take on the task of 'saving civilization'.[1] Given that the poets in question were politically conservative this in practice meant saving civilization from the barbarians. For Eliot, 'the hooded hordes swarming/Over endless plains', threaten both the achievements and future of western culture. 'Falling towers/Jerusalem Athens/Vienna London'. If we ask who exactly these hordes are, the answer seems to be: those who have brought about and/or who constitute the new mass democracies and, perhaps, newly created democratic nation states, from Communist Russia through, say, the Weimer Republic to Ireland-in-the-making. On 7 April, 1921, Eliot wrote a deeply instructive letter to Richard Aldington, in the course of which he confessed that

> Having only contempt for every existing political party, and profound hatred for democracy, I feel the blackest gloom. Whatever happens will be another step towards the destruction of Europe. The whole of contemporary politics oppresses me with a continuous physical horror like the feeling of growing madness in one's brain. It is rather a horror to be sane in the midst of this, it is too dreadful, too huge for one to have the feeling of superiority. It goes too far for rage.[2]

It is not clear what event or events Eliot has especially in mind

---

To avoid littering the text of the essay with unnecessary references I have given beside relevant quotations the titles of all poems by Gurney and Rickword to which I refer. They can then be consulted in *Collected Poems of Ivor Gurney*, chosen, edited and with an introduction by P.J. Kavanagh, London, O.U.P. 1982, and *Edgell Rickword: Collected Poems*, ed. Charles Hobday, Manchester, Carcanet, 1991.

[1] I have borrowed this phrase from Lucy McDiarmid, who takes it as the title for her excellent book on 'Yeats, Eliot, and Auden Between the Wars,' Cambridge, C.U.P., 1984.

[2] The letter is quoted by Donald Davie in *Poetry Nation Review* May/June, 1991, p. 24

as advancing 'the destruction of Europe.' The previous year, dockers at Tilbury had refused to load arms which the government had promised Poland and white Russia; but although Eliot would have been dismayed by the dockers' success in forcing Lloyd George to back down from the promise to which Churchill and others had committed him, that was now in the past. So too were the revolutions in the defeated axis powers of Germany and the Austro-Hungarian empire. A free Ireland? But in April 1921 that was still far from certain.[3] These occurrences may have helped form Eliot's 'blackest gloom', but it is more likely that he is thinking specifically of England and its growing industrial unrest, particularly among the miners, the railwaymen and the transport workers.

There were good reasons for this unrest. In 1920 the government had announced plans to hand back to mine and railway owners those essential industries which had been under state control during the war years. The date set for the re-privatisation of both mines and railways was August, 1921, but according to Henry Pelling,

> the heavy losses being made by the coal industry led [the government] to advance the date of transfer of the mines by five months. The coal owners for their part could see no alternative to heavy cuts in wages, which of course the Miners refused to accept. The result was that on the day of decontrol, 31 March, the Miners were locked out and the Triple Alliance was again invoked. The Railwaymen and the Transport Workers agreed to begin a sympathetic strike on Saturday, 16 April . . .[4]

In the event the railwaymen backed down and created what in Labour history is known as 'black Friday'. The General Strike of May, 1926, would be an attempt to make good the damage done to the Labour movement by the failings of April 1921. It, too, failed. But I am fairly certain that the strike was instrumental in helping Eliot's decision to take out British citizenship, and to announce that he was a royalist, anglo-catholic and conservative.

[3] In his *Ireland 1828–1923: From Ascendancy to Democracy*, Oxford, Blackwell, 1992, D. George Boyce remarks that although by the end of March 1921 the government was under increasing international and internal pressure to resolve the Irish question – especially in the light of the Black and Tans' brutal tactics – 'the cabinet felt it had no option but to stand its ground and meet war with war' p. 99.
[4] Henry Pelling, *A History of British Trade Unionism*, Harmondsworth, Penguin, 1963, p. 165.

Eliot himself acknowledged that 1926 was a key year. When he closed down *The Criterion* with the coming of the second World War, he wrote an editorial farewell in which he remarked that

> Only from about the year 1926 did the features of the post-war world begin clearly to emerge – and not only in the sphere of politics. From about that date one began slowly to realize that the intellectual and artistic output of the previous seven years had been rather the last effort of the old world, than the struggles of a new.[5]

He would presumably have regarded *The Waste Land* as belonging to a last effort of the old world. These fragments I have shored against my ruins.

Eliot finished his great poem in December 1921. That same year Yeats published *Michael Robartes and the Dancer*. The volume includes 'Easter, 1916' and 'The Second Coming'. In the former Yeats broods over the 'terrible beauty' of the blood sacrifice and what it foretells about the making of an independent Ireland. 'The Second Coming' is also about the creation of a new society, even a new world order. Here, however, Yeats is far less equivocal. 'Mere anarchy is loosed upon the world'. The perpetrator of anarchy is of course the famous beast out of Revelations. 'And what rough beast, its hour come round at last,/Slouches towards Bethlehem to be born?' The poem has been the subject of much commentary, most of it concerned with Yeats's 'Vision': that is, his reading of history as consisting of two-thousand year cycles in which one kind of civilization passes into its opposite. I want merely to note that the rough beast which 'slouches' must surely be the working class. We know that shortly after the October revolution in Russia Yeats began a (re) reading of Wordsworth's poetry at the same time as he was re-reading Burke on the French Revolution; and in his copy of *The Prelude* he marked some lines of the 1850 text of books X and X1 which deal with the Revolution. In the first of these Wordsworth speaks of 'The indecision on their part whose aim/Seemed best, and the straightforward path of those/Who in attack or in defence were strong/Through impiety,' (ll. 130–133); and in the second, very famous passage, he tells of how he himself lost 'all feeling of conviction, and, in fine,/Sick, wearied out with contraries,/Yielded up moral questions in despair.' (lls 302–305). These two moments find

---

[5] Quoted by Samuel Hynes in *The Auden Generation: Literature and Politics in England 1930s*, London, Faber, 1979, p. 33.

an obvious echo in the lines of 'The Second Coming': 'The best lack all conviction, while the worst/Are full of passionate intensity'.[6] But who are the worst? Those who make revolutions? Very probably. Political radicals, then, even communists? Quite likely. For though in 'Easter, 1916' Yeats acknowledges the worth of Pearce and Connolly, he knew that both were communists; and the 'blood-dimmed tide' of 'The Second Coming' may well catch up the events and aftermath of the Easter Rising as well as the Bolshevik rising and, then, assassination of the Czar and his family. Communists and their sympathisers and radical allies are 'Leaders of the Crowd', Helens of 'social-welfare dream,' or dreamers of 'some vague utopia.' As such, they let loose 'a roof-levelling wind,' which threatens to destroy everything that stands in its way, including, of course, 'monuments of unageing intellect'. In ranging promiscuously among a number of poems which Yeats wrote in the post-war period I mean to do no more than point towards how thorough-going was his commitment to identifying the enemies of civilisation as the champions of mass democracy. *This* was what history had let loose, and it was from *this* that civilization had to be saved, even if such salvation had to be accomplished within the pages of a book. There, if nowhere else, could be the celebration of 'beautiful lofty things.'

II

Eliot was American. Yeats was Irish. What of the English? Older English poets were either finished, no good, or so traumatised by the war that they had nothing to say either to or about the post-war world. This is also a widely-accepted view. Robert Bridges' 'Low Barometer' was the nearest any of them came to confronting or at least trying to negotiate a sense of the post-war world (dis) order. In that poem there is to be found at least some recognition of the horrors that have wrecked the cherished dream of England as the great, good place. Gone, perhaps forever, is the 'record of the long, safe centuries,' to use Henry James's formulation.[7]

[6] For this see an article by Patrick J. Keane on Burke, Wordsworth and the Genesis of 'The Second Coming' in *Bulletin of Research in Humanities*, New York, Spring, 1979.
[7] The phrase comes from *Within The Rim* – the title of both essay and book – which James wrote shortly after the outbreak of the Great War.

> Some have seen corpses long interr'd
> Escape from harrowing control,
> Pale charnel forms – nay, ev'n have heard
> The shrilling of a troubled soul,
>
> That wanders till the dawn hath cross'd
> The dolorous dark, or Earth hath wound
> Closer her storm-spredd cloak, and thrust
> The baleful phantoms underground.

Bridges' fear of those baleful phantoms explains his endorsement of closer ties with the defeated nations, for which *The Times* gave him a verbal battering. But the faded diction and strict metres of 'Low Barometer' all too plainly speak from and for an older world. They voice a last, desperate, unavailing effort to keep under control the nightmare vision of a world given over to death.

Bridges apart, the older generation of poets is most importantly represented by Hardy who, when Robert Graves visited him in August 1920, was supposed to have told the younger man that English poets would have to continue 'writing on the old themes in the old styles, but try to do a little better than those who went before.' I have set out elsewhere my reasons for doubting that Hardy said any such thing, but whatever the truth of the matter there can be no doubt that the words have been used against both him and later English poets, including those who were at work in the 1920s and of whom Sidney Bolt remarks that 'the themes of these poets were too new to be accommodated by minor modifications of the style they inherited.'[8]

Bolt does not say which poets he has in mind, but they could include any number of those whom Edward Marsh included in his *Georgian Poetry 1920–1922*. All the usual names are there: Abercrombie, Blunden, W.H. Davies, de la Mare, Graves, Harold Munro, Robert Nichols. Lawrence's 'Snake' has also slipped in, but looks to be very much the intruder in this otherwise pre-lapsarian collection of English poetry in which it is all-but impossible to find any mention of a recent war. Reading through the anthology is a very odd, disturbing experience; and it must have been even more so in 1922. It is as though Marsh is hoping to persuade his audience

---

[8] For this see my essay on New Polyolbions in *Critical Dialogues: Current Issues in English Studies in German and Britain*, eds. Isobel Armstrong and Hans-Werner Ludwig, The British Council/Gunter Narr Verlag, Tübingen, 1995.

that the age-before-last survives intact. Nothing of importance has happened betwen the first of his anthologies, which he had put together in 1912, and now. Faced with Marsh's anthology and the kind of poetry it champions – which it has to be said went on being produced in large quantities during the post-war years – it is not difficult to see why literary historians have come to regard the 1920s as a blank page in the annals of English poetry. There simply wasn't any.[9]

Or rather, none of it deserved serious consideration. As the decade went on it became possible to see that a trio of poets killed in the war would in all probability have been the major writers of the post-war years. But with Owen, Rosenberg and Edward Thomas all dead, who was left? The answer seemed and has continued to seem to be: Blunden, Graves and Sassoon. I am not going to deal with them here, beyond saying that as officer poets they found the war a deeply disturbing experience: not primarily because of the inevitable horrors of trench warfare but because the experience called into question most of the the beliefs and allegiances which they had acquired through their class, education and upbringing, and none of them could bear to follow where the questions led. Blunden wrote a number of poems that look back on the war as a dystopic experience: a time of wrecked pastoral. Then he went back to writing pastoral poems. Sassoon was for a while a socialist. He contributed to *The Daily Herald*; he spoke on party platforms; and in one poem he diffidently expressed support for striking miners. But the setting of that poem is his Gentleman's Club; and Sassoon honestly admits that, hearing his 'port-flushed friends discuss the Strike' he would almost like/To see them hawking matches in the gutter.' 'Almost': the wry shame-facedness of that looks towards the characteristic note of his autobiography, *Sherston's Progress*, published in 1936, by which time Sassoon had long abandoned his socialism.

In a poem-review of Sassoon's autobiography, Hugh MacDiarmid asks 'What is *Sherston's Progress* but an exposure/Of the eternal Englishman/Incapable of rising above himself,/And traditional

---

[9] *The Calendar of Modern Letters* savaged most of the collections that came from The Poetry Bookshop and/or which found favour with Squire. As a result, the journal sometimes give the impression of denying the worth of any specifically English poetry produced in the post-war period. Siegfried Sassoon, for one, wondered why it must always be attacking everything.

values winning out/Over an attempted independence of mind . . . It is not that Sherston was either/A weak or cowardly person./It is rather that his rebelliousness was only/Superimposed on his profoundly English nature'.[10] By 'profoundly English nature,' MacDiarmid means, I think, a willing and/or finally unquestioning obedience or conformity to class and national expectations. England expects. Sassoon had once and bravely confronted those expectations. By making his famous protest against the continuation of the war he risked court-martial and execution. He was saved from the consequences of his action by the intervention of friends.

Pre-eminent among them was Robert Graves. We know that Graves, like Blunden and Sassoon, was severely traumatised by his war experiences. In later years he suffered recurrent nightmares and during the 1920s his mental condition was often precarious. By the end of the decade he had had enough. He wrote *Goodbye To All That* and with Laura Riding left England for Majorca. Once there, he tried his hand at a play called *But It Still Goes On*. This has no merits as drama but forms a kind of apologia in which the hero, Dick, at one point talks of his sense of a catastrophe, of 'the bottom dropping out of things.' This is how he explains it:

> perhaps one easy way of describing the catastrophe is to say that it was the moment when the last straw broke the back of reality, when one unnecessary person too many was born, when population finally became unmanageable, when proper people were finally swamped. Once they counted; now they no longer count. So it's impossible for a proper person to feel the world as a necessary world – an intelligible world in which there's any hope or fear for the future – a world worth bothering about – or, if he happens to be a poet, a world worth writing for – a world in which there's any morality left to bother about, but his own personal morality: *that* gets more and more strict, of course.[11]

---

[10] For a fuller account of MacDiarmid's criticism see my essay on Sassoon in Lucas, *Moderns and Contemporaries*, Brighton, Harvester Press, 1985.
[11] Robert Graves, *But It Still Goes On*, London, Cape, 1930, p. 293. In *Robert Graves: His Life and Works*, London, Hutchinson, 1982, Martin Seymour Smith – pp. 208–210 – reveals that Graves had been commissioned to write a play and that although he knew nothing about the stage accepted the commission because he and Laura Riding needed money to build a house on Majorca. I have no reason to query the truth of this, and this is no doubt why the play is choc-a-bloc with Graves' preoccupations of the moment.

The Nietzschean contempt for little people and belief that mass democracy takes away function from that 'proper person', the poet, is Graves's own right enough, although Laura Riding's influence is plain to see. (Before coming to England she had been briefly involved with 'Fugitive' poets and shared their Southern scorn for democratic politics.)

In short, the soldier poets who survived the war found themselves unable or unwilling to try to explore its meaning or the contradictory experiences to which it had exposed them. They can hardly be blamed for this. But their decision to seal the war off from their consciousnesses will explain why we continue to look to Eliot and Yeats for deep, authoritative (and authoritarian) readings of the post-war world. There are no other poets to whom we can turn.

III

Except that there are. Both Ivor Gurney and Edgell Rickword fought in the war and both survived it, although at great cost. Gurney, who had a history of mental disturbance which the war exacerbated, was from 1922 until his death in 1937 shut away in asylums, first in his native county of Gloucester, and then at Deptford, Kent. Rickword was wounded and after the war began to suffer from nightmares which lasted until his death in 1979. Both were poets, Gurney a great one. Both were politically radical – although in Rickword's case this has been said to have put an end to his poetry (it didn't), and in Gurney's case it has been largely ignored by the few commentators he has so far attracted. Yet Gurney's radicalism is bound up with his war experiences and is integral to his best poetry. Rickword's came later. His move from post-war discontent to left-wing politics happens over a long period and *may* be connected to the fact that, like Blunden, Sassoon and Graves, he was an officer. Gurney wasn't. And this is of the greatest possible significance.

To see why we have only to look at one of Gurney's finest war poems, 'The Silent One.'

> Who died on the wires, and hung there, one of two –
> Who for his hours of life had chattered through
> Infinite lovely chatter of Bucks accent:

> Yet faced unbroken wires; stepped over, and went
> A noble fool, faithful to his stripes – and ended.
> But I weak, hungry, and willing only for the chance
> Of line – to fight in the line, lay down under unbroken
> Wires, and saw the flashes and kept unshaken,
> Till the politest voice – a finicking accent, said:
> 'Do you think you might crawl though there: there's a hole.'
> Darkness, shot at: I smiled, as politely replied –
> 'I'm afraid not, Sir.'

There are certain issues in these lines to which I shall return, but for the moment I want to note that the 'finicking accent' clearly belongs to an officer, whose exquisite politeness is such that he disguises a command as a question. No question mark follows 'Do you think you might crawl through there: there's a hole.' But the line-soldier can play the game of pretending to answer a question. Hence, 'I'm afraid not, Sir.' The capitalisation of Sir alerts us to the politeness which Gurney takes good care to retain in this exchange with the officer. Nevertheless, he is rejecting the officer's claim to authority. He has no wish to be a hero, a noble fool. Yet it doesn't seem enough to call Gurney's attitude anti-heroic. A better word might be 'bolshie,' not in the sense that Gurney comes across as sullenly unresponsive – he smiles, replies politely – but in the sense that 'bolshie', which entered the language at this time, was used to mean 'left-wing, unco-operative, recalcitrant.' (I quote from the O.E.D. definitions.)

Words come into existence because they are needed. Bolshie defined a new consciousness. And the coupling of left-wing with unco-operative implies that co-operative people are right-wing or at least support the status quo. In war that has to mean obeying the orders of your superiors, no matter how daft or murderous those orders might be. As officers, Owen, Graves and Sassoon had to give orders to their men; and at a shrewd guess all of them possessed what the men would regard as 'finicking accents.' We are told that all three officer-poets were much admired, even loved by the men they led, and there is no reason to doubt the truth of this, nor to question the more general claim that an emotional bonding often developed between line soldiers and their serving officers. They were after all equally exposed to hardship and danger. And yet Gurney's 'bolshie' response to the voice of authority in 'The Silent One' serves to remind us that while officers might well think of the war as one with which they ought to be at ease or to which they should be reconciled – it was what their education had prepared them for – the rankers had far less reason to accept it. For them, the war inceasingly became 'the bosses' war.'

'The Silent One' was never published in Gurney's lifetime. It seems to have been written in 1919, by which time publishers had turned against his poetry, perhaps because they no longer wanted war poems, and very probably because they sensed in Gurney an attitude that did not accord with simple statements of duty and of patriotic pride. They could hardly have missed it. Yet to call it an attitude is to imply that Gurney is merely 'bolshie', and this is far from the truth. It is rather that as a poet-survivor of the war he becomes the spokesman for 'boys who served time overseas', as he says in 'Mist on Meadows', who 'could not guess, alas!/How England should take as common their vast endurance'. 'Where are they now?' he asks in another poem, and replies

> on state-doles, or showing shop-patterns
> Or walking town to town in borrowed tatterns
> Or begged. Some civic routine one never learns.
> The heart burns – but has to keep out of face how heart
>   burns. ('Strange Hells')

The masterly use of enjambement between the second and third lines intensifies the terrible indignity of those many returned soldiers who were forced onto the dole or into a vagrant life. And I take it that by the civic routine one never learns Gurney wishes to direct us to the bitter irony of ex-soldiers who had fought to make 'a land fit for heroes' and who now offend against 'decency' by their beggarly appearance. (In passing I should note that officialdom wanted to keep badly injured soldiers from attending the dedication of the Tomb to the Unknown Soldier, on the grounds that their presence would lower the dignity of the occasion.) Nor can the 'boys' risk showing their bitterness or anger, not anyway if they hope to gather a crust or a stray penny. They must instead learn 'to keep out of face how heart burns.'

But the heart is also Gurney's, his anger the anger of those with whom he had fought and whom he now sees as cast off by the very nation on whose behalf they had vastly endured suffering. This is crucial. Gurney's anger springs from political consideration. An attentive reading of his letters makes plain that during the war years he had moved towards an increasingly politicised awareness of what he hoped for from post-war society. Letters he wrote during 1917 to his great friend Marion Scott show this beyond any doubt. This is not to suggest that key events of that year were decisive in turning him towards political radicalism. They may have had that effect but, lacking as we do a proper biography, much in Gurney's intellectual development remains a mystery.[12] We do, however, know that shortly after hearing of the Kerensky revolution he wrote to Marion Scott to tell her that 'it is the bloomingest nuisance that a thing so well intentioned as the Russian Revolution can so upset things.' He does not explain what the upset is, but it is reasonable to suppose that he would have had in mind Allied distrust of the democratising of their Eastern ally. Two months later he tells Scott that England suffers under a 'wrong materialistic system'. Again, he does not explain the remark but the the context suggests he has in mind the vulgar wealth which had been so dominant a presence in pre-war England, his dislike of which lies behind a remark contained in a letter of the previous year, in which he tells her that 'the people here say that France was very happy and well-governed before the War. Can you imagine an Englishman saying as much of England?'

Then, on October 16, 1917, comes a key letter. Gurney begins by reassuring Marion Scott that he hadn't intended her to take personally a sonnet 'To the Prussians of England' which he had enclosed with his previous letter. This is the sonnet.

> When I remember plain heroic strength
> And shining virtue shown by Ypres pools,
> Then read the blither written by knaves for fools
> In praise of English soldiers lying at length,
> Who purely dream that England shall be made
> Gloriously new, free of the old stains
> By us, who pay the price that must be paid,
> Will freeze all winter over Ypres plains.
> Our silly dreams of peace you put aside
> And Brotherhood of Man, for you will see
> An armed Mistress, braggart of the tide,
> Her children slaves, under your mastery.
> We'll have a word there too, and forge a knife,
> Will cut the cancer threatens England's life.

---

[12] Michael Hurd's *The Ordeal of Ivor Gurney*, Oxford, O.U.P, 1978 is a first attempt at a biography of Gurney but is notably lacking in information about Gurney's intellectual development and his social/political affiliations.

Scott, who seems to have been innocently patriotic and a good 'hun-hater', must have been disturbed by Gurney's dream of an international Brotherhood of Man and his rejection of Britannia as a warrior-nation. But I suspect she was most deeply shaken by the promise of violence with which the sonnet ends. And after all, for Gurney to write in *October 1917* of forging 'a knife' to cut England's 'cancer' – when it is plain that by 'cancer' he means the ruling class – could hardly be taken as other than revolutionary.

In trying to justify himself, and at the same time assuage her fears, Gurney explained that he cared 'more for Englishmen, than for liberty of England.' And in order to explain *that* remark, he adds:

> It is of more importance that the Duke of Bilgewater should respect and sympathise with Bill Jones than that the sun should never set on the British Empire, whose liberties have been kept alive by revolt against the fathers of the present 'Prussians of England.'[13]

Gurney's respect and sympathy for Bill Jones is intimately linked to his relishing of the salty speech of the soldiers with whom he fought, their idiomatic expressions, their various dialects. In several letters he quotes stray remarks he has overheard, of 'infinite lovely chatter'. And the poems rejoice in the speech of line soldiers. Their utterances, both what they say and how they say it, are revelations of wit, warmth, *aliveness*, which makes the class assumption of authority so much malign, ignorant nonsense. To take two examples. In the first of two poems called 'First Time In' Gurney recalls 'roguish words by Welsh pit boys/ . . . sung – but never more beautiful than under guns,' and in 'Billet' he tells of the private in the Glosters who

> took on himself a Company's heart to speak,
> 'I wish to bloody hell I was going to Brewery – surely
> To work all day (in Stroud) and be free at tea-time – allowed
> Resting when one wanted, and a joke in season,
> To change clothes and take a girl to Horsepool's turning,
> Or drink a pint at 'Travellers Rest' and find no cloud.

This savouring of the speech of line soldiers prompts or makes possible that political vision, that intense desire for democratic

[13] Quotations come from *Ivor Gurney: Collected Letters*, ed. R.K.R. Thornton, Manchester, Carcanet, 1991, pp. 261, 288, 348, 151 and 352–4.

relations, which partly accounts for Gurney's 'bolshieness', but which, far more importantly, is the source of much of his best work. Here, then, we need to register the importance to Gurney of Edward Thomas.

When Gurney heard of Thomas's death he told Marion Scott 'This is a great loss.'[14] But at the time he seems to have known few if any of Thomas's poems. By autumn, 1917, however – that key period in his life – he is beginning to weigh their significance. And by the early spring of 1918 he is able to provide one correspondent with a long list of Thomas's poems he particularly likes and to tell another that Thomas is a genius. In March 1918 he writes to Marion Scott that his own future poetry is likely to be 'influenced by E.T. chiefly.'[15] Thomas did indeed come to be a pervasive influence on Gurney's poetry, although in ways that mostly lie beyond the confines of this essay. Thomas's socialism is, however, a different matter. With the honourable exception of Stan Smith, commentators have chosen to ignore Thomas's politics, even though he himself said that 'Except William Morris there is no other man whom I would sometimes like to have been', and even though he makes plain that his admiration for Morris has to do with the fact that for Morris 'poetry was not, as it has tended more and more to be in recent times, a matter as exclusive as a caste. He was not half-angel or half-bird, but in all that he did a man on terms with life and toil, with the actual troublous life of every day, with toil of the hands and brain together...'[16]

I have no means of knowing whether Gurney had read *The South Country*, from which that quotation comes. I suspect he had, but like so much else to do with Gurney we still lack information about his reading. We do, however, know that in August 1918 he told his friend Haines that he had started to learn 'Lob' by heart, that he wished Thomas 'had written piles of stuff more,' and that 'some day the prose works will (I hope) delight me likewise.'[17] Lob, Thomas's tutelary Englishman, is the embodiment and spokesman for English liberties. 'Nobody can't stop 'ee. It's/A footpath right enough.' These are the words of the free-born Englishman, carrying

---

[14] *Collected Letters*, p. 249.
[15] See *Collected Letters*, esp. 391–441 passim.
[16] Edward Thomas, *The South Country*, London, Dent, Everyman, 1993 edn., p. 87.
[17] Gurney, *Collected Letters*, p. 441.

with them natural authority that belongs with the speech of place, of belonging. P.J. Kavanagh says that 'when there are people in [Gurney's] poems they are seen with rather an abstract, lonely, passion of respect.' This may sometimes be the case, but I have given examples – and they could be multiplied – of Gurney not merely seeing but *hearing* those people; and their utterances put flesh on the bones of respect, 'prove' it, to use a word Thomas himself favoured. And it is therefore worth remarking that Gurney wondered why Thomas 'doesn't break out into divine unliterate clearness more often?' He reported a 'Snatch of Shakespearean wit, from Pte Tim Godding. A sergeant was going round collecting birthdays . . . and one man hesitated to answer. Said T.G. 'He don't know his birthday, he don't know his name. The sun hatched it.' And of *The Dynasts* he said that it was 'quite Shakespearean . . . O the country talk, the songs.'[18]

As to Lob. The man was wild/And wandered,' the narrator of the poem is told. By the time Gurney came across 'Lob' he had already written his own 'Song': 'Only the wanderer/Knows England's graces,/Or can anew see clear/Familiar faces.' He enclosed this lovely poem in a letter to Marion Scott of January 1917 and it appeared in the first of the two volumes to be published in his lifetime, *Severn and Somme*, 1917. (*War's Embers* followed two years later). In retrospect he must have come to regard wandering as part of his heritage as a free Englishman; and he would have understood that Thomas is using the word to carry the same political weight that it bears in Blake, Wordsworth and Clare. Wandering is a right because the land is what we have, or ought to have, in common.

After his return to England, Gurney became an inveterate wanderer, even a compulsive one. His wandering is both a Thomas-like eagerness to look, to know, to 'bite the day to the core', and an affirmation of an Englishman's rights. And these are not merely country rights. The poet who wrote 'One comes across the strangest things in walks' ('Cotswold Ways') also wrote 'North Woolwich,' which begins with Gurney looking down at the smoky squalor of the dockside Thames, and reflecting on the fall this represents from 'the bright/ Morning of new Time amongst tall derricks/And floating chimney pots with empty tackle/Drawn by fierce asp-things slowly out of sight.' The forced image of asp-like tugs is there to underline a contrast between twentieth-century Thames and the pristine beauty of the

---

[18] See *Collected Letters*, pp. 12–13 and *Collected Letters*, pp. 382, 70 and 486.

ancient mediterranean, of 'Hellene memories' and 'Sappho's easy happy mirth.' So far, so inconsiderable, even inept. Poems that contrasted times when the world was new to now, when it has grown old, and grey and weary, had been ten-a-penny ever since Wordsworth's sonnet 'The world is too much with us.' And Wordsworth knew rather more about Triton than Gurney does about Sappho.

But Gurney's poem then turns from conventionalities to the quite startlingly original. The last section begins with what looks like another routine contrast between ancient Spartan youth and the present decadent city-bred young who lack 'that smoothly running muscle'. The poor physical condition of the working-class had become a much-canvassed matter of concern in late nineteenth-century England; and it was accompanied and/or prompted by debates about degeneration of the stock.[19] But Gurney is not bothered about *that*.

> Gaol waits for them would face without a stitch
> Heaven's nakedness, those feet are black as pitch
> Should gleam on gold sands white or in stadium lines.
> Can Aphrodite bless so evil dwelling
> Or Mercury have heed to Canning Town?
> Nay, rather, for that ugly, that evil smelling
> Township, a Christ from Heaven must come down,
> Pitiful and comradely, with tender signs,
> And warm the tea, and shield a chap from fines.
> A foreman carpenter, not yet full-grown.

East End missions were a feature of Christian socialism from the middle years of the nineteenth century. But this is something else. This workingman Christ, 'on close terms with life and toil, with the actual troublous life of every day,' is 'comradely'. Gurney's use of the term will owe something to Whitman, whose poetry he knew and deeply admired. It will also owe something to that close bonding between trench soldiers on which I have already commented and which, as Paul Fussell and others have suggested, is often marked

---

[19] The best discussions of this murky subject are to be found in William Greenslade's essay on Fitness and Fin de Siècle in *Fin de Siècle/Fin du Globe*, edited by John Stokes, Macmillan, 1992 and the same author's full-length study of the concept of degeneration at the turn of the century, published by Cambridge University Press in 1994.

by homo-eroticism.[20] But Gurney's use of the word 'comradely' is at once more social and political. The Pagan Gods can do nothing for modern London. Christ, the foreman carpenter, can.

Or can he? If the poetry is in the pity Gurney feels for London's working-class youth, then the politics are seeded in the recognition that comradeship is what will save them, will 'warm the tea, and shield a chap from fines.' Christ the carpenter is an image of such comradeship but only in so far as he is a working man, 'not yet full-grown.' For by that last phrase I take Gurney to mean that those who become more than foreman grow away from comradeship. They become bosses, separated from 'toil of the hands and brain together.' And it is this separation which Gurney opposes. His socialistic convictions have much in common with Morris and for that matter with the Tolstoyan belief in the redemptive power of physical labour, where that is an expression of what Morris's master Ruskin called 'the full man.' And like both Morris and Tolstoy Gurney fears the city as a place of degrading labour – 'useless toil' Morris called it – and therefore of degraded men and women. Work here is not so much with the hands as by the 'hands'. That is why London is a place of 'evil dwelling.' And it is why, in a later poem called ' A Wish' he begins : 'I would hope for the children of West Ham/Wooden-frame houses square, with some sort stuff/Crammed in to keep the wind away that's rough,/And rain; in summer cool, in cold comfortable enough.'[21]

Gurney wrote 'A Wish' sometime after his terrible breakdown in the autumn of 1922. This may explain the lines in which he voices a wish for the children of West Ham to have houses with plots of land where they might

> use spade or the hand
> In managing or shaping earth in such forms

---

[20] I know nothing of Gurney's sexual proclivities. The letters indicate that while in war-time France he became briefly engaged, but the identity of the woman remains a mystery. In *The Great War and Modern Memory*, Paul Fussell has written well of the homo-eroticism of some war poetry but I do not see Gurney's work as particularly homo-erotic, unless we cite the dubious evidence of 'To His Love'.
[21] It may be that Gurney had in mind the dreadful poverty of Poplar, which had led to the imprisonment in 1921 of George Lansbury and the Labour Councillors of the district. They refused to levy rates which they knew their constituents could not meet.

> As please the sunny mind or keep out of harms
> The mind that's always good when let go its way
> (I think) so there's work enough in a happy day.

As he well knew, there was not enough work for millions of men who had fought in the war and who were now reduced to 'state-doles, or showing shop-patterns/Or walking town to town.' And he himself was jobless, despite repeated attempts to find work. To be sure, he found it difficult to hold any work down, but there is in his poetry at this time a passionate desire to celebrate what he calls in 'The Lock Keeper' 'A net of craft of eye, heart, kenning and hand.'

'The Lock Keeper' is Gurney's 'Lob.' Not so great a poem, but a very fine one. There is no space here for the lengthy discussion the poem merits, but I need at the very least to remark Gurney's statement that 'to praise men' is 'still a luck and a poet's privilege.' And the man *he* praises 'goes in my dark mind/ ... Might well stretch out my mind to be a frame – /A picture of a worthy without name.' The matter-of-factness with which he mentions his own 'dark mind' is as noteable as his feeling that such a mind could be 'stretched' to fit, like a picture frame, the full portrait of the anonymous lock keeper. The lock keeper is any and everyman, like Lob, in fact. And also like Lob he is a tutelary spirit: a countryman, a man of craft, cunning, and one who is free to wander, to work, and to 'talk with equals', among whom are included 'coalmen, farmers, fishermen his friends/And duties without beginnings and without ends.' This man does not work by the clock, is not a hired 'hand'. He is in short the embodiment of that Morrisian dream of the truly free man.

That Gurney yearned for such freedom with its necessary if paradoxical-seeming commitment to work – of 'hands and brain together' – is evident from a number of remarkable poems, all of them written between 1919 and 1922. There is, for example, the following, which I quote in its entirety.

> The hoe scrapes earth as fine in grain as sand,
> I like the swirl of it and the swing in the hand
> Of the lithe hoe so clever at craft and grace,
> And the friendliness, the clear freedom of the place.
>
> And the green hairs of the wheat on sandy brown.
> The draw of eyes towards the coloured town,
> The lark ascending slow to a roof of cloud
> That cries for the voice of poetry to cry aloud.

The echoes of Thomas ('Tall Nettles' and 'Digging') and of Housman's 'coloured counties' do not so much detract from this lovely lyric as help secure its sense of a perfect harmony momentarily achieved in and through labour. In 'The Valley Farm' Gurney speaks of how the woodchopper 'in the sun/Moves with such grace peace works an act through him,' and as with 'The Hoe Scrapes Earth' and 'The Lock Keeper', man, work and landscape are brought into a kind of visionary harmony which is to be found in some of Thomas's poems and is, of course, celebrated in Vaughan Williams' 'Lark Ascending'. (Gurney's use of the title as a phrase in 'The Hoe Scrapes Earth' is an instinctive act of homage to the contemporary composer whose work meant most to him.)

The same harmony prevails in 'Felling a Tree.' 'The surge of spirit that goes with using an axe,' that wonderful poem begins; and it ends with the tree finally cut down:

> The axe fell from my hand, and I was proud of my hand,
> Crickley forgave, for her nobleness, the common fate of trees
> ... the tree that for long had watched Wales glow strong,
> Seen Severn, and farm, and Brecon, Black Mountains times
>   without reckon,
> And tomorrow would be fuel for the bright kitchen – for brown
>   tea, against cold night.

As with 'North Woolwich', so here: 'brown tea' has an almost sacramental value for Gurney because it is linked to what it may seem doctrinal to call productive labour and yet for which I can find no other useable term.

Gurney worried that his own insecurely-followed professions of musician and writer were far from productive. His career as a composer was stalled and although his two wartime volumes had sold reasonably well he couldn't get anyone to publish a third collection of his poems, to which he had given the title *Rewards of Wonder*. Given his uncertain mental condition it isn't at all surprising that he should have come to feel desperately unsure of himself. But the poem 'Hedger', written in the autumn of 1922, rejects self-pity. It begins with a mingling of hand and brain: 'To me the A Major Concerto has been dearer/Than ever before, because I saw one weave/Bright patterns of green.' Art is redeemed, illuminated, by the craft of the hedger, whom the wandering Gurney tries to assist. 'But clumsy were the efforts of my stiff body/To help him in the laying of bramble, ready/Of mind, but clumsy of muscle in helping,' whereas 'his quick moving/Was never broken by any danger, his loving/Use of the bill or scythe was most deft, and clear.' Faced with such skill, Gurney is forced to think about his own work as a musician:

> Had my piano-playing or counterpoint
> Been so without fear
> Then indeed fame had been mine of most bright
>   outshining;
> But never have I known singer or piano-player
> So quick and sure in movement as this hedge-layer
> This gap mender, of quiet courage unhastening.

Gurney's readiness here to make himself ridiculous – his acknowledgment of how he was 'clumsy of muscle' – is not mock modesty. His unawed certainty of the hedger's skill merely acknowledges the craft of hand and eye. And while praise of the man's 'quiet courage unhastening' seems at first excessive we may well feel on reflection that it pays its way. At all events, Gurney's recognition of the hedger's calm methodical ability to cope with recalcitrant material goes with the humbling acknowledgment of his own failings; and it ensures his refusal to consider the artist as innately superior to the artisan, to separate him off from those who are his fellow men, fellow workers.

This wish not to be separated comes out even more strongly in 'The Mangel-Bury', which must have been written at very much the same time as 'Hedger'. The poem begins with Gurney coming across a carter filling his cart with mangels, joins him in his work and 'We threw them with our bodies swinging, blood in my ears singing.' That last phrase is redeemed from cliché by the emphatic internal rhyme that records and celebrates this seized moment of utopian harmony. But then he and the man separate: 'my pain to more moving called/And him to some barn business far in the fifteen acre field.' By 'my pain' Gurney must mean the terrible mental distress that forced him into those endless walks, by night as by day, about the Cotswolds, and which also expressed itself in the paranoid delirium which would lead to his institutionalisation. And we can then gauge the intensity of his distress when we note how the poem opens: 'It was after the war; Edward Thomas had fallen at Arras – /I was walking by Gloucester musing on such things/As fill his verse with goodness.'

For Gurney saw himself as taking over from Edward Thomas, of becoming the poet who celebrates the troublous life of every day. And even more than it had been for Thomas, Gurney's was a peopled landscape. It was also more local, and more deeply known. I cannot here follow his intimate acquaintance with 'my two thousand year home,' as he called the Gloucestershire country through, across and around which he walked; nor can I do more than suggest that his post-war poetry is much concerned with what would now be called Green Politics. But it must at least be said that Gurney's imagining a 'Golden Age' of England's past to be situated in Elizabethan England, where he claims there was 'some/Natural moving towards life's love/ ... men working freely.../... On a free soil' ('The Golden Age'), is less a soft-focus appeal to some routinely conceived mythic past than a strategy as useful as Morris's appeal in *A Dream of John Ball* and *News from Nowhere* to a 'merrie England' which operates as utopian contrast to capitalist class-separations and the progressive de-skilling of workpeople.[22] For Gurney as for Morris and Thomas, England was to be most fittingly imaged as a field full of folk. And Gurney's loathing of the invasion into the fields of bungalow and villa has to be understood, not as snobbishness, but as fear of what happens to a society which loses contact with its history. As he says at the end of 'The Bargain':

> Waltheof's field will become a rubbish heap.
> Villas will stand there and look polite; with folk polite
> Where sedges stood for the wind's play and poet-delight,
> But Severn will be sorry and it can never be right.

Poet-delight is here, as so often in John Clare, for that congruence of nature and element, sedges and wind, which intimates a sanctioned

---

[22] *Merrie England* was the title of Robert Blatchford's work, first published in his socialist newspaper, *The Clarion*, in 1893, then in book form for the first time the following year. In this widely-read and frequently reprinted work, Blatchford, an avowed disciple of Morris, sets out an account of the blight of capitalism on the lives of workers and offers a socialist alternative. I find it difficult to imagine Gurney hadn't at least heard of Blatchford's book, and his own version of a genuine 'merrie England', which he locates in Jacobean times, is, for all its ahistoricality, important for his acute understanding of the ways in which Shakespeare and other dramatists of that period draw on common speech and idiomatic expressions and of how they image an England remarkable for its 'whole' living. It should be noted that between 1900–1914 several Arts and Crafts communities established themselves in the Cotswolds.

propriety of relationship only to be broken at terrible cost. At the end of 'Possessions', a lament over the cutting down of trees for the War, Gurney says 'It was right for the beeches to stand over Whitcombe reaches,/Until the wind roared and softened and died to sleep.' Internal rhyme indicates a harmony of relationship which affirms its being right. The word 'right', with its clear implication of natural rights, is no more casually invoked than it is when Clare uses it to protest against the depradations of aggressive individualism.[23]

But as we have seen, Gurney's post-war experiences disabused him of his war-time hopes that in England such rights would be championed and might even succeed in toppling the Duke of Bilgewater and his kind. At the time of his breakdown he wrote 'Sonnet – September 1922,' a dark, impacted poem in which a terrible sense of defeat seems to be battling it out with whatever hope he retains for men working freely on a free soil.

> Fierce indignation is best understood by those
> Who have time or no fear, or a hope in its real good.
> One loses it with a filed soul or in sentimental mood.
> Anger is gone with sunset, or flows as flows
> The water in easy mill-runs; the earth that ploughs
> Forgets protestation in its turning, the rood
> Prepares, considers, fulfils; and the poppy's blood
> Makes old the old changing of the headland's brows.
>
> But the toad under the harrow toadiness
> Is known to forget, and even the butterfly
> Has doubts of wisdom when that clanking thing goes by
> And's not distressed. A twisted thing keeps still –
> That thing twisted easier than a grocer's bill –
> And no history of November keeps the guy.

I do not pretend to fully understand this poem. But in the first eight lines Gurney seems to be saying that those who have the energy to protest against injustice are those who enjoy indepen-

---

[23] Gurney's concern with such rights cannot be disentangled from more general fears of the despoliation of England in the post-war period, a matter taken up by Clough Williams-Ellis in a book called *England and the Octopus*, which, when it was published in 1928, was enthusiastically reviewed by D.H. Lawrence, whose own attacks on 'ugliness' in his writing about Nottingham and the Mining Villages and in a famous passage of *Lady Chatterley's Lover* are also germane.

dence or who nurture confident dreams of the future. Yet whether they do so or not, history rolls on and over them and they are sacrificed as it advances. In the sestet we have either to read toad and butterfly as compliant with their fate, and of no more importance than a paper spill used to start a conflagration – a Guy Fawkes' bonfire; or that they protest against their fate but are destroyed by superior forces. Bleakly terrible though this reading is, it does at least keep open the possibility of protest. It also allows us to sense how deeply Gurney felt the outrages committed on his fellow men by the post-war government, that government's mute, cynical denial of responsibility for any social and political vision, its ready toleration of mass unemployment among those who had fought 'the bosses' war.' And although I do not doubt that Gurney's experiences as a soldier had exacerbated his already precarious mental balance, it is surely demeaning to a great poet not to acknowledge how in the period 1919–1922 his imagination was seized by the violence he saw being done to his hopes for a just society – hopes he must have shared with many thousands of other soldiers. Out of such hopes he made poetry. Out of the defeat of those hopes he made more poetry. And the poetry he made offers a decisive rebuke to any reading of post-war writing which claims as unopposable the authoritative voices of Eliot and Yeats.

IV

A year before Gurney was shut away Edgell Rickword published his first collection of poems, *Behind The Eyes*. Like Gurney, Rickword had fought in the war. Unlike Gurney, he was an officer. A few of his war poems find their way into most anthologies. After demobilisation he entered Oxford intending to study French. He lasted at the university for no more than a year and then set out for London and a life of literary journalism. *Behind The Eyes* contains a number of fine love poems, a witty farewell to Oxford ('Complaint of a Tadpole Confined in a Jam-Jar'), and is characterised by an air of at best fastidious melancholy:

> Whilst now in dusky corners lovers kiss
> and goodmen smoke their pipes by tiny gates –
> these oldest griefs of Summer seem less sad

> than drone of mowers on suburban lawns
> and girls' thin laughter, to the ears that hear
> the soft rain falling of the failing stars.

The exquisite note of ennui is however debilitating.

Rickword's next volume, *Invocation to Angels and The Happy New Year* was published seven years later. (The collection is more often known as *Invocation to Angels* but as will become apparent later the full title is important and should be retained.) Some of the earlier poems in this collection would not be out of place in *Behind the Eyes*. But there are new strengths, as here, in 'Luxury.'

> The long, sleek cars rasp softly on the kerb
> and chattering women rise from cushioned nests,
> flamingo-tall, whose coral legs disturb
> the mirror-surface where creation rests . . .
>
> The churches' sun-dried clay crumbles at last,
> the Courts of Justice wither like a stink
> and honourable statues melt as fast
> as greasy garbage down a kitchen sink.
>
> Commercial palaces, hotels de luxe
> and Banks in white immutable ravines,
> life's skeleton unfleshed by cynic rooks,
> remain to warn the traveller what it means . . .
>
> Time has no pity for this world of graves
> nor for its dead decked out in feathery shrouds.
> The ghoul must perish with the flesh he craves
> when stars' hoarse bells of doom toll from the clouds.

According to Charles Hobday, 'Luxury' had its origins in a visit Rickword paid to Paris in the summer of 1924.[24] This may well be so, but the poem as we have it mingles vision and prophecy in order to speculate about the hidden but sensed decadence of city life – *any* city; and this hints at a larger, more inclusive decadence. It is therefore of immediate relevance to note that at the time he was writing 'Luxury' Rickword was considering setting up the literary magazine which, when it began publication in 1925, would be called *The Calendar of Modern Letters*, and that, as Arnold Rattenbury has

---

[24] Charles Hobday, *Edgell Rickword: A Poet at War*, Manchester, Carcanet, 1989, p. 24.

rightly commented, contributors to *The Calendar* were aware that they were attacking ' a largely moribund literature, and increasingly the issue was posed as to whether this was not because the whole of society producing it was moribund.'[25]

By no means all the poems included in *Invocation to Angels* can be read as sophisticated, mordant comments on contemporary society. But the most ambitious project of the volume, 'The Happy New Year', most certainly can; and Rickword himself clearly saw this 'Masque' as of signal importance. Hence, his including its title in the title he gave to his volume. And this must, I am certain, be connected to the fact that the masque was written between the spring and autumn of 1926. Rickword therefore was working on 'The Happy New Year' throughout the period of the General Strike and its immediate consequences. This needs to be pointed out, because otherwise we might be tempted to think that Rickword's real concern is the war and its aftermath. The evidence for this concern lies partly in the fact that Rickword chooses as epigraph for his masque some lines from Jasper Heywood's play, *Thyestes*, which takes for subject the murder by an uncle of three young nephews and his serving them to the boys' father. This provides an apt allegory of the butchery of a generation during 1914–18. The London setting of 'The Happy New Year' can therefore appropriately enough – though with a bow in the direction of *The Waste Land* – modulate into a phantasmagoric landscape of war: 'A fog-like poison drifts and whirls/such dreadful faces as the sun shone on/lying in fields, propped against walls, on beds/mottled with leaf-lights.' These are the dead of no-man's land but also of the contemporary city, where 'I had not thought death had undone so many.' (And although Eliot's image derives from *The Inferno*, it may also have been prompted by footage of war-film showing soldiers in their thousands slogging up the line to death.)

To say this brings me to what Hobday calls 'a very curious paragraph' in the issue of *The Calendar* for April 1926. Here, the unnamed writer, whom Hobday thinks must be Rickword, speaks of a poem which the editors have procured and in which 'the crops rot, the land becomes water-logged, and complete sterility ensues. The author considers this an adequate symbol of the contemporary

---

[25] Quoted by Hobday, *Edgell Rickword*, p. 102. For more on the *Calendar* see Hobday, esp. chapter 6, and my essay on Edgell Rickword in *The Sewanee Review*, vol. CII, no. 1, 1994, pp. 112–121.

consciousness ... literary references are intended to enrich the texture of the verse with imagery, for invention risks being vulgar, and, besides, the success of several very cultured poems has recently approved the innovation.'[26] It may be, as Hobday suggests, that Rickword initially intended his poem to be a burlesque on *The Waste Land*. The masque makes use of a city setting and a mythological sub-structure. In a prefatory note Rickword explains the action as spanning the course of the year, from the moment when the sun 'falls through the celestial map (of the Ptolemaic system) from the zenith through the astronomical signs, Houses, to the no-where below the Arctic horizon.' The sun then 'retraces his steps and sequentially injects his vigour into the earthlings dwindling from his absence. This perigrination is observed with detachment expressed in an ironic commentary by the Sinisters who finally dissociate themselves.'

The tone of this suggests that Rickword stands at an ironic distance from his own scheme. It may even suggest that he is not at all sure how seriously he wants his masque to be taken. If so, that can only be because he is distrustful of poetry which uses myth as a way of foreclosing on the complexities of history – including the history of the present. In his opening speech, the Presenter provides a melange of faded poetic styles and mannerisms, ways of speaking about the falling/failing sun:

> Rosy-slippered dawn
> goes tripping down the spangled lawns
> but drab reminders dun insolvent streets ...
> where moribund the later sons of earth
> bask and chew up the remainders of their days,
> contemning Sol's archaic ways
> whose heaped bonfire in the romantic style
> nurtures their candle-end of wit and wisdom.

There is no telling whether this is the sun of empire, of western civilisation, or of hope briefly aflare after the armistice. Most likely it is meant to suggest all these things. But now in 'the wall-eyed city' the Presenter announces that 'Sol falls weakly through his ruined house,/a dead coal in a rusty grate.'

Rickword was a member of the Labour Party. This does not mean that Sol's weak fall can be read as an allegoric statement of

---

[26] Hobday, *Edgell Rickword*, pp. 96–7.

MacDonald's first, brief, ineffectual administration; but in 'The Happy New Year' the Presenter speaks of those brave hopes which have foundered because of 'vows rescinded, broken contracts,' and of the many who 'renounce complaints in wan waters' or who 'fall on pity's sword.' Their choice is between suicide and the death of self-regard. At which point, with wonderful inappropriateness, the Chorus intones 'London has many merciful instruments,' and the Presenter then speaks of these 'withered souls . . ./with bands of music wailing through the streets.' This is followed by the direction (*Here the Sinisters come on.*) Hunger marches, marches of the unemployed, of strikers: these are all implied in the 'bands of music', as are the street bands of former soldiers. This is London, 1926.

And in this London 'The sunny side of the road/crawls with the aged like a lousy seam.' As a soldier himself, Rickword knew all about lice. Here, they function as relics of a discredited generation who, in a newly-risen sun (the defeat of the strike?) continue to bask in wealthy comfort and who include among their number such literary coteries as are unwilling to confront the political-social issues of the time. So at least I read the Presenter's next lines, indicting 'An embryo with dim reptilian brain/womb-bound in Wandsworth, and the female flocks/from dullest Kensington, and City ants and owl-wise Bloomsbury, [who] all send up a shout.' They are joined by the 'Dexters' who must surely be the Bright Young Things, for in their chorus they sing

> We do not crave eternity
> love's bowl of quintessential pearl,
> since half an hour's propinquity
> exhausts the meaning of a curl,
> but hail one Blessed Trinity,
> The Time, the Place, and a Girl.

The Sinisters, however, although they briefly assent to the triumph of the newly-risen sun, do so on different terms. 'New blood begets new forms/for comedies or tragic shows,/new vigour to confront old storms.'

Rickword's revival and adaptation of masque as an example of new form has then to be seen in the light of his review for the *Calendar* of Enid Welsford's *The Country Masque* where, as Hobday points out, he speaks of masque as developing from ' a rough, licentious ritual,' and as having as its primary impulse the celebration or inducement of 'fertility and felicity.'[27] In 'The Happy New Year' the Chorus's last lines are: 'Like begets like, immortal in each kind;/through perishing units'union, death's defeat.' Units may die, but in union lies ultimate victory. The failure of the general strike was due to the collapse of union solidarity and, as the strikers saw it, the caving-in of union leaders before Baldwin's ambiguous and soon disowned promises. The choice of masque form for 'The Happy New Year' makes evident Rickword's intent to connect emergent political and social energies with new or at least revived and adapted cultural modes of expression.

Not that the masque ends on a note of triumph. After the Chorus's promise of death's ultimate defeat the Presenter makes a sombre concluding speech:

> I see others who walk the earth tonight, homeless
> throughout the city, pacing day's void suburbs
> by unmade roads, raw gardens, blank-eyed lamps,
> cinders and tin-cans and blown evening papers,
> among refuse-pits and sewer-mouths,
> wandering fires and voices of the swamp;
> passing deliberately into the night
> through the infinite extension of this landscape.

These lines powerfully blend images of contemporary London with an infernal Dantean landscape, where the poor who pass 'deliberately into the night' may be seen as offering a future threat to the sunny side of the road. Hobday quotes from a review of Trotsky's pamphlet, *Where is Britain Going?*, which appeared in the *Calendar* in July 1926. The reviewer, whom Hobday thinks may have been Garman, poses the question as to whether 'there exists a proletarian party to take advantage of the position of contemporary social malaise. The answer to it will decide whether England ... is to stay on the road of continually degenerating values, or to create a revolution as vital, potentially, as the inception of Christianity.'[28] For Rickword an achievable Happy New Year lies in the future and his masque is an at once sardonic and deeply unsettling vision of contemporary sociey. And as with Gurney, so with Rickword: the prospect which filled Eliot with 'the blackest gloom', was for them lit by the sun of an achieved democratic state.

[27] Hobday, *Edgell Rickword*, p. 99.
[28] Hobday, *Edgell Rickword*, p. 95.

Paul Muldoon: The Annals of Chile
CLAIR WILLS

> The ghost of Roger Casement would now call 'enough'
> to the claymore and Kalashnikov
>
> and, lest the green
> flag should come to stand chiefly for gangrene
>
> or some corrosive bile,
> would join me in one last appeal
>
> to our Irish-American cousins: let them show
> they heard what Gerry Adams said only weeks ago –
>
> that 'there's a need to end
> all acts of violence': let them send
>
> a clear signal to the President of Sinn Fein
> that *his* clear signal wasn't sent in vain –
>
> now that the living outnumber the dead
> we ought to quit while we're still ahead.

PAUL MULDOON'S WORK has become well known for its quality of formal control, the tight rein it draws on expressivity and emotion, and its tone of ironic detachment from the confusions and particularities of politics and history. What are we to make then of the very 'unMuldoonian' poem, 'A Clear Signal', which was published in the *New York Times Review of Books* on St Patrick's Day 1992? The poem was written following the debacle of the 'X' case in Ireland, which concerned the Irish State's initial refusal to allow a fourteen year old alleged rape victim to travel to England for a termination of her pregnancy. The Supreme Court finally ruled that the girl's threatened suicide overruled the guarantee (inserted into the Irish Constitution after the 1983 referendum) of protection for the life of the unborn. The case caused an outcry which nearly brought down the Reynolds government, and eventually was instrumental in causing an alteration to the laws on freedom of information about abortion services in England.

This seems to be a straightforwardly political, and indeed interventionist poem. Muldoon presents his views as pro-abortion, pro-lesbian and gay rights, and anti-repression. But at the same time he suggests that contemporary Irish culture is more 'forward' and liberal on these issues than an increasingly right-wing and fundamentalist United States (where for example the pro-abortion judgement of Roe vs. Wade is under attack). Indeed he calls on the Irish-American community to abandon its violent conservativism – symbolised both in the refusal to allow Irish lesbians and gays to march in the annual New York St Patrick's Day parade, and in the inflammatory rhetoric of Noraid. Paradoxically he suggests that Irish Americans might learn from indigenous Irish republicanism which (particularly with the Hume-Adams talks) shows greater flexibility than its 'globalized' version.

In 'A Clear Signal' Muldoon portrays Ireland as a country coming out of 'backwardness' and into enlightenment, where enlightenment means life-giving 'flexibility' rather than gangrene or corrosive bile. Moreover in the mention of Roger Casement, he hints at a history of nationalist politics in Ireland which foreshadows contemporary sexual pluralism, although such dissident sexualities remain hidden and unacknowledged. At the same time Muldoon undercuts a teleological narrative of progress, by suggesting that in America 'modernity' has brought intolerance and repression for women and sexual minorities rather than enlightened attitudes.

In keeping with this emphasis on the 'private' realm of sexuality as an index of modernity, the poem suggests that Ireland's 'crisis' is not so much, or not only, the civil war in the North, but the crisis caused by the clash between conservative religion and modernity in the whole island. While this association of sex and violence may be familiar from Muldoon's previous work, particularly 'The More a Man has' and 'Madoc-A Mystery', in *The Annals of Chile* the critique of the links between masculine violence and power in both its imperialist and anti-imperialist guises is more explicit. Just as the work resists the easy identification of a narrative of progress from backwardness to maturity, it also opposes the idea of a move from 'traditional' national homogeneity to contemporary cosmopolitan heterogeneity. Muldoon has always stressed the heterogeneous nature of 'Irishness', marked not only by a complex history within Ireland and in the Irish diaspora, but also by shifting political and personal allegiances – determined as much by desire and self-interest as religious or national ideals. In Muldoon's Ireland sexual and national identifications both were and are various, though their variety is fiercely denied and repressed.

Throughout *The Prince of the Quotidian* and *The Annals of Chile*, consideration of the relation between Irish history – the national ghosts of the past and the violent present (which like Joyce in *Dubliners* Muldoon images as 'the dead') – and the contemporary world is filtered through a reflection on the 'globalization' of Irishness, particularly its Americanization. In 'A Clear Signal', the line 'Now that the living outnumber the dead' suggests advance and development, but as I have suggested Muldoon puts no trust in the idea of historical progress from tradition to enlightened modernity[1]. 'Now', rather than a cause for celebration, here acts as a warning of the need to avoid a recurrence of violence. Both the ostensible theme of *Annals* (a consideration of the significance of childhood events for the grown man), and the extraordinarily complex, intercut and repetitive structure of the long poem 'Yarrow' are part of a meditation on the process of learning both personal and political lessons from history. How by turning back and for ever replaying the past, might it be possible to create an alternative future? How can one turn the repetition of 'the same' into something different?

The Globalisation of Everyday Life

In the villanelle 'Milkweed and Monarch', Muldoon offers the 'butterfly effect' as an image of global interconnection. The symbiotic relationship of his parents, now merged in the grave, is naturalised as the special relationship between plant and insect, or the interdependence of global weather systems as 'a wing-beat' in America 'may trigger off the mother and father/of all storms, striking your Irish Cliffs of Moher/with the force of a hurricane'. But in addition to such cause and effect (which is of course political and economic as well as natural), one way to think about the process of globalization, particularly in relation to media technology, is as the repetition of cultural phenomena in different contexts (like the background setting of 'Yarrow' where Muldoon watches, among other things 'a Spanish *Lear*' on Cable T.V. in 'a den in Newfoundland'). Throughout *The Prince* Muldoon meditates on the inter-

---

[1] The reference here is to the fact that there are now apparently more living people on earth than have ever died in the history of humanity.

section of global networks of communication and culture, and the (banal) elements of everyday life, asking when the person who experiences this life, seemingly uprooted from cultural context, becomes 'different'? This can be read as an extension of earlier challenges by Muldoon to the self-contained, 'national', character of the public sphere. Networks of communication and exchange are no longer bounded (if they ever were) by a national community with identifiable members; instead they are characterised by anonymous flows of information, and driven by economic forces. But so far from suggesting that this experience of globalisation is altogether 'post-modern', Muldoon uses it as an image through which to reflect on the contradictory status of progress and modernity. He sets up a contrast between contemporary, media-led internationalism and an eighteenth century version of globalism. Scattered throughout these volumes are references and allusions to eighteenth century Irish revolutionary figures (such as Wolfe Tone and Bernardo O'Higgins), who attempted to translate enlightenment ideals from one part of the globe to another and to realise universal (or global) ideals of liberty and democracy within a particular nation-state. But the traffic between the old and the new world was not only freighted with enlightenment concepts, and Muldoon also presents us with Irish figures engaged in exporting the catholic counter-reformation to Spanish dominions. As 'A Clear Signal' suggests, the point of Muldoon's exploration of these historical and geographical connections is to reflect on the complex relationship between 'backwardness' and 'progress'. This is in large part what is going on in the 'parallel' he draws between Ireland and Chile.

The link between Ireland and Chile first appears in the 'diary' sequence, *The Prince of the Quotidian*. The sequence 'records' the events of the 31 days in January 1992, charting both the gestation of his child (who was born in July of that year), and the first inklings of his long poem 'Yarrow'. This 'January journal' differs from much of Muldoon's work, in that the poems are very clearly dealing with 'quotidian' encounters, events and actions, as well as exploring everyday rhythms of speech and thought. At the same time, however, the poems derive shape by maintaining the formal composition of sonnets, rhyming triplets, couplets and so on. Rhyme becomes an almost subliminal structuring element, as 'mulch' rhymes with 'Milosz', 'MLA' with 'homily', and 'parachute' with 'Saint Brigid'. Partly these rhymes are simply funny, but they also serve to give the poems a conversational feel, which is emphasised too by the colloquial diction.[2]

As one reviewer has noted, the fact that these are 'diary' poems is ironically signalled in the first poem, with the appearance of Frank O'Hara, seemingly offering some advice on modes of transport, gleaned from his own death by beach-buggy:

> Yet another wore a caul
> made from a beach-towel edged with a blue flower;
>
> 'Try,' he said, 'try not to confuse *carrus*, a cart,
> with *carina*, a keel . . .'

This piece of advice is offered as Muldoon and his wife leave Manhattan through the Holland tunnel. Within the tunnel under the river their vehicle is something between car and boat, or it floats between the elements, as another poem puts it, of 'surf and turf'.

In keeping with the metaphor of a journey, *The Prince of the Quotidian* is also an exploration of narrative form, as each poem leads into or refers to others in the sequence. In large part this is achieved through formal echoes, and in particular Muldoon's use of half-rhyme. So the carina of the above lines becomes 'ocarina', and later 'Corinna'. Through such echoes, the poem sequence meditates on the tension between arbitrary or random linguistic differences, and grounded or rooted meanings[3]. The transformation of one thing into another is partly determined by the vicissitudes of language, and partly through imaginative association. For example the image of a ship or keel (carina) is taken up several times during the poem sequence, through the idea of 'anchoring'. One poem asks how meaning is anchored or held firm in the context of a global, 'everyday' poetry in which elements are gleaned from diverse contexts, with little seeming organisation going into the composition. Employing the characteristic Muldoonian trick of offering contradictory 'advice' on how to read it, the poem offers an ironic apology

---

[2] It is worth noting here the development in Muldoon's use of the idea of a 'private language'. In comparison with the poem 'Quoof' for example, here markers of particularity are not so much familial, or regional, but those of gossip and the 'in' crowd. Nicknames (such as 'Mike' Keeley, or 'Coleslaw' Milosz) are signalled by inverted commas, suggesting that it is important for us not to miss the careful construction of a particular closed social discourse.
[3] Compare the earlier treatment of these concerns, for example in the poem 'Sushi'.

for the 'trivial' nature of the poem sequence, and at the same time suggests that for some this randomness has purpose:

> none will,
> I trust, look for a pattern in this crazy quilt
> where all is random, 'all so trivial',
>
> unless it be Erasmus, unless
> Erasmus again steel
> himself as his viscera are cranked out by a windlass
>
> yard upon 'xanthous' yard;
> again to steel himself, then somehow to exhort
> the windlass-men to even greater zeal.

Here the reformation figure Erasmus becomes anchored by his own intestines, suggesting that the body is indeed a vessel in which to undertake a journey – whether carrus or carina. This poem suggests that anchorage is physical and indeed physiological, but the sequence as a whole reflects on the function of family and community in grounding the individual. Family connections are also partly physical of course, as the corporeal link with the mother reminds us. While *Annals* seems concerned above all with a reworking of the history of Muldoon's childhood, as well as to a lesser extent his more recent past, *The Prince of the Quotidian* takes on childhood in another fashion, in charting the gestation of Muldoon's own offspring.

Of course the body of a pregnant woman is indeed a vessel for another, and this theme is echoed in the poems in *Annals* which are concerned with the birth of Muldoon's daughter. In 'The Birth' the umbilicus becomes a form of anchor, and the nurses on duty during the caesarean section are 'windlass-women'. Here the question of being in or out of 'one's element' is concentrated on the border between inside and outside the mother's body. In a more general sense the poem seems to be asking about 'belonging'. In what sense does childhood 'anchor' you – give you an identity in the flux of contemporary global culture? How far do origins within a particular family, culture and national history determine the future? In addition, part of the spur to Muldoon's consideration of these issues is, as I will discuss below in relation to 'Yarrow', a fear of the *repetition* of familial history. In becoming a father will he reproduce not only a child, but the structure of his own childhood?

To refer back to the discussion of historical globalisation, and Muldoon's suggestion that the late twentieth century is not necessarily more enlightened than the eighteenth, here the related concern is about whether the contemporary father can become different, can progress.

The Prince begins with the borrowing of a bassinet, and the baby is increasingly 'realized' throughout the sequence – as we are given the visual image of the foetus on an ultrasound scan, the prospective birthdate, and the fact that she is female. Later he 'can hardly refrain' from letting slip her chosen name, Dorothy Aoife, in a telephone conversation. It is in relation to the baby's due date that the idea of the relationship between a significant date in Northern Ireland's 'replaying' of history and the 'annals of chile' is first introduced:

> That our child's due date is the Twelfth of July –
> the anniversary of the birth of Neruda
> but a red-letter day in El Norte
> rather than Chile –
> is an irony that won't escape
> the famous Longalley or the famous Montagael

The reference here is to the poets Michael Longley and John Montague, though of course this irony won't now escape any of us, since he so carefully points it out.

The link between 'North' and 'South' is forged throughout the poem sequence in the details of everyday life, as well as more pointed historical markers. For example, one of the activities that Muldoon and his wife are engaged in during January is leafing through holiday travel literature on Louisiana and the Southern States. Such reading (as well as visual images in still photographs, film and video) serves to transport the reader across time and space. At one point Muldoon is 'translated' to the west of Ireland:

> As I coasted into the tunnel
> of the Pennington car wash
> I glanced at my copy of *Feis*
> By Nuala Ni Dhomhnaill
>
> a wave broke over a rock
> somewhere west of Dingle;
> my windshield was a tangle
> of eel-grass and bladderwrack.

As in *The Annals*, (where it's boy's adventure fiction, epic and romance), it's the very old-fashioned pastime of reading which makes the world contract in this way. Reading – as well as more recent modes of communication such as film and T.V. – can obliterate cultural distances, but at the same time create experiences of tremendous force and local particularity. The 'cafe of the world' created through travel literature, cookery, film and television, is thoroughly postmodern, but Muldoon suggests that it can be enriching too. Despite its long historical pedigree, reading is part of this postmodern experience to the extent that it stands in for actual travel, 'authentic' or 'first hand experiences' of other places and cultures. (One could argue indeed that this simulation of authenticity has always been the function of literature). But as Muldoon says 'this new quotidian' harbours quaint ironies, and it is naturally these that interest him. The poem brings together the idea of 'visiting' the south through travel literature, the contraction of the contemporary world, with the idea of rootlessness – and a favourite Muldoon theme, betrayal. Muldoon distances himself from the statement contained in the poem by saying he 'heard' rather than thought it:

> 'Let him,' I heard, 'let him be one ignited by the quaint
> in this new quotidian: a mound
> of coffee beans in the 'Cafe du Monde';
> the New Orleans School of Cookery's
> okra-
>
> monious gumbo; a dirigible of Paul Prudhomme
> floating above the Superdome;
> let the Prince of the Quotidian lead an alligator
>
> along the banquette of Decatur
> yet let him not, with Alejandro O'Reilly,
> forget the cries of the bittern and the curlew.'

Written on the birth of his Irish-Canadian nephew, this is a picture of global 'Irishness', which Muldoon seems to be presenting as yet another 'variety of Irishness'.[4] With international 'flavour' part of his formative experience, the child's identity will not be defined by narrow national, ethnic or religious boundaries. But what is the

---

[4] See Roy Foster, *Modern Ireland* (Penguin, 1989), 3–14.

significance of the reference to the eighteenth century figure O'Reilly here? Is Muldoon suggesting that the Irish disapora has anticipated the contemporary globalization of culture? that 'modernity', in the guise of dislocation and national fragmentation, has been an element of Irish experience for centuries? There is, I think, a more specific point at issue here. As Muldoon has repeatedly stressed, particularly with reference to Native American histories, the Irish diaspora cannot be understood only as a modern or postmodern condition, but needs to be placed in the context of its roots in the seventeenth and eighteenth centuries – hence his frequent gestures towards historical links between the old world and the new through trade, colonisation, exile, and of course the figure of the mercenary. The Scots Irish mercenaries who fought on all sides during the Indian Wars in America are familiar from 'Madoc'. Similarly Alejandro O'Reilly was an Irish mercenary who fought for the Spanish in the mid 18th century, and was rewarded with the governorship of Cuba. From there he invaded Louisiana and repressed New Orleans on behalf of catholic Royalist Spain.

One of the ways you might choose to read this emphasis on powerful anti-Republican Irishmen in the new world, is as a criticism of an exclusive emphasis on the figure of the Irishman or woman as victim or exile. And Muldoon certainly has things to say about this. In a characteristically double-edged way, he offers as his epigraph for the book a passage (again from the 18th century) detailing Wolfe Tone's 'exile' in Princeton (where Muldoon now teaches). And at the same time Muldoon rejects the suggestion that as a poet he is exiled in the States, instead transposing the idea of exile to rural Northern Ireland ('I'm not "in exile",/though I can't deny/ that I've twice been in Fintona.'). Again, partly what is at issue here is a question of how the poet is 'grounded', what should be his 'element' within the global system. At the same time Muldoon undercuts the idea that exile and alienation from the community comes only with travel and geographic displacement. Fintona, a small town in Co. Tyrone became renowned throughout Ireland in the nineteen fifties following a documentary film, made partly in secret, exposing organised discrimination against catholics (particularly over housing).[5] Indeed, throughout *The Prince* and *The Annals*

---

[5] See Kevin Rockett, Luke Gibbons and John Hill, *Cinema and Ireland* (London: Routledge, 1989), 81–2.

of Chile, Muldoon suggests that the experience of being 'at home' is always also one of internal exile.

In a larger frame, Muldoon is clearly concerned with the ways that a self-consciously 'Irish' identity becomes absorbed into larger 'global' formations. This is of course a familiar preoccupation of his – how things can be 'the same' and yet distinct because placed in different cultural, political, or indeed linguistic, contexts. Muldoon might have chosen to present the cultural differentiations *within* global Irishness as a tension between cosmopolitanism and rootedness, but he undercuts this opposition by using birds, so often a symbol of flight, as his image of 'home'.[6] The bittern and curlew, like the corncrake, have tremendous resonances in Irish literature (and despite their 'global' feel both *The Prince* and *Annals* are very bound up with old Irish literary texts). The cries here are those of 'The Yellow Bittern', an 18th century poem which partly reflects the bitterness born of the experience of post-plantation Ireland.[7] Is it then that O'Reilly, in becoming a royalist mercenary, has forgotten the political lessons – of repression and dispossession – that he should have learned in Ireland?

As I have argued Muldoon is exploring not only the legacy of enlightenment in Ireland and America, but also the 'counterprogressive' forces of conservative and repressive catholicism. His latest work thus focuses on concerns similar to those in 'Madoc – a Mystery'. But 'A Clear Signal' acts as a reminder of the fact that the conflict between these two historical forces has not only resulted in sectarian violence in the North of Ireland, but also repression of women within the family. At the end of *The Prince*, the Muldoon figure has begun to learn this lesson. The talking horse who appears in the final sections, in his likeness to Achilles' horse Xanthus, reminds him of his mortality and insists: 'you must atone/for everything you've said and done/against your mother'. In this very specific way *The Prince* serves as an introduction to the 'feminine' concerns of *The Annals of Chile*.

---

[6] In order to make his journey back 'home' to Ireland in 'Yarrow', Muldoon is transformed into a bird.
[7] Cathal Bui Mac Giolla Ghunna, 'The Yellow Bittern', in *The New Oxford Book of Irish Verse*, ed. Thomas Kinsella (Oxford, 1986). The same 'bibulous bittern' appears in the closing lines of 'Yarrow'.

Unapproved Roads

Muldoon presents us with a map of global connections, both historical and contemporary. The links he explores are not so much those between the centre and the periphery, the metropolis and the colony, but instead are those lateral journeys or 'unapproved roads' between Ireland and cultures such as those of the Native Americans, or South America which in themselves have a complex history of colonisation and – in the case of Chile – violent independence. It is clear too, that he is interested not only in how familial (maternal) and national origins may define or 'ground' the individual who uproots himself through exile or emigration, but also how the global system ensures that you are always elsewhere even when you are at home.

'Brazil' is a poem deeply concerned with such questions of time and space, as well as femininity. 'Brazil' is at once Brazil – the South American country, and Hy Breasil, the Isle of the Blest. Here, as in 'Immrama' and other poems in his earlier volume *Why Brownlee Left*, the land of the blest becomes associated with South America, but now it is the mother rather than the father who becomes imaginatively connected with it:

> When my mother snapped open her flimsy parasol
> it was Brazil: if not Brazil,
>
> then Uruguay.
> One nipple darkening her smock.
>
> My shame-faced *Tantum Ergo*
> struggling through thurified smoke.

In a lecture he gave at the literary festival in Hay-on-Wye in 1994, Muldoon commented on his long-standing imaginative association of his childhood home with a South American hacienda, an association forged partly through the pampas grass which grew near the house, and which has come to signify for him a crystallisation of memory and childhood. (As one reviewer noted, as much as those of Chile, these are the annals of childhood):

> This image of the 'pampas', or as it appears in another poem, 'That hacienda's frump/of pampas-grass' ('The Earthquake') is particularly evocative for me. There was, in our garden, a great 'frump' of pampas-grass that has, for me, come to stand for something along the lines

of Eliot's 'rose-garden' from the opening section of 'Burnt Norton':
> What might have been and what has been
> Point to one end, which is always present.
> Footfalls echo in the memory
> Down the passage which we did not take
> Towards the door we never opened
> Into the rose-garden.

It seems that this 'pampas-grass' includes not only an idea of 'what might have been' but some notion of 'what might yet be'.[8]

This blessed land, the farm, the home is bound up with both maternal sexuality (the mother's body) and catholicism (the thurified smoke, the font) with all its prohibitions. It is the concatenation of the two which embarrasses him. The poem charts an imaginative transformation of home into South America, the far east, the south seas:

> Later that afternoon would find
> me hunched over the font
>
> as she rinsed my hair. Her towel-turban.
> Her terrapin
>
> comb scuttling under the faucet.
> I stood there in my string vest
>
> and shorts while she repeated 'Champi . . . ?
> Champi . . . ? Champi . . . ?' Then,
>
> that bracelet of shampoo
> about the bone, her triumphant 'champiNON'.

Objects become 'exoticised': 'Her towel-turban./Her terrapin/comb scuttling under the faucet.' French Mushrooms become Spanish (or possibly Portuguese?), signalling a similar process of 'translating' words and concepts from the old to the new world. In keeping with this, the mother, and the home are represented as opening out to the rest of the world. So far from being a restrictive influence the mother here acts as a route into the exotic, the far away. This is

---

[8] 'Between Ireland and Montevideo', The First Waterstones Lecture, May 29th 1994, Hay-on-Wye Festival of Literature. Subsequent prose quotations from Muldoon will be taken from this lecture.

partly because the mother is associated with reading, and therefore transportation to other worlds. One might recall here Muldoon's earlier representations of the ideal childhood moment – for example the poem 'Bran', which constructs a nostalgia for purity which has become corrupted by adult sexuality in the metropolis. In contrast, here the exotic world of erotic pleasures and adventure fiction is located within the family.

The poem is in part a consideration of what things are and what they are not (though this is not Brazil, and not Uruguay it might have been – the imagination has the power to transform the everyday into the exotic). 'ChampiNON' shouts prohibition, but the mother's body is an arena of desire nonetheless. (This is confirmed by the bracelet of shampoo, recalling Donne's bracelet of hair by which his love will be revealed even in the grave):

> If not Uruguay, then Equador:
> it must be somewhere on or near the equator
>
> given how water
> plunged headlong into water
>
> when she pulled the plug.
> So much for the obliq-
>
> uity of leaving *What a Boy Should Know*
> under my pillow: now *vagina* and *vas*
>
> *deferens* made a holy show
> of themselves. 'There is inherent vice
>
> in everything,' as O'Higgins
> would proclaim: it was O'Higgins who duly
>
> had the terms 'widdershins'
> and 'deasil' expunged from the annals of Chile.

What are we to make of this movement from top to bottom, the slippage from chest to genitals, paralleled with the 'vas deferens', the pipe leading down from the sink? The first two sections of the poem reveal glimpses of the upper body, the breast – the nipple, and the chest through the string vest. The last section suggests that such nakedness is a displacement for concerns with the lower body as 'vagina and vas deferens made a holy show of themselves' – they made an exhibition of themselves, but also perhaps they revealed themselves while remaining veiled or holy? There are connotations here of the underworld (vice), but borders are also at issue here. The translation of top into bottom parallels the 'translation' of North into South, or position on the border, the equator, between the northern and southern hemispheres. Space is collapsed as, for a moment, the place which mother and son inhabit in this poem is neither north or south. In one way this may be because they are catholics in the North, and much of 'Yarrow' is taken up with the mother's attempt to distance herself from the ungodly rack and ruin she sees around her in the North. But I think one thing to note about the poem is the fact that the North is not absorbed into the South, or the other way around. Instead it is through an imaginative leap that the difference between North and South ceases to exist – and this on both a national and a global plane. Bernardo O'Higgins, like Alexandro O'Reilly, was an Irishman 'translated' into the southern hemisphere (or son of such a man, Ambrosio O'Higgins – who was both a mercenary fighting for Spain, and later Governor of Chile). O'Higgins was partly educated in England, where he became imbued with the ideals of republicanism and enlightenment, and later fought the Spanish to become leader of an independent Chile. He thus 'translates' liberty into Spanish, brings it from the old to the new world. Clearly O'Higgins represents an alternative to O'Reilly here, and also perhaps offers a blueprint for a son looking for a way not to reproduce in the image of his father. O'Higgins overturns the work of his father in the service of Catholic and Royalist Spain, and introduces enlightenment ideals into the new Chilean Republic, even taking action against Catholic ritual and superstition. He 'bridges the gap' between North and South.

In addition to the sudden disappearance of the border, the poem also imagines the redundancy of left and right, as the circling of water in either direction is overridden by gravity. 'Widdershins' and 'deasil' mean turning to the left and to the right, anti-clockwise and clockwise. There is a link here with 'Yarrow', for, as Muldoon tells us in the long poem, the name of the local seed merchant Tohill's (which figures highly in the poem) is the anglicisation of Tuathal, 'meaning withershins – with its regrettable overtones of sun worship'. But lurking in there is the etymological sense of 'North' (tuaidh), and, not surprisingly 'south' too (deisceart). The North is therefore associated with turning to the left, and the South with the right. The implication is perhaps that the North has gone astray, has turned the wrong way, worships the wrong gods. This interpretation is backed up by the figure of the mother in 'Yarrow'.

Her concern throughout the poem is to keep her son on the right moral and religious track, and to insulate him from the culture around him, though the child Muldoon is forever 'taking off' in other, less worthy, directions. In 'Brazil' the mother represents *both* opposing forces, left and right, leading to a moment of stasis and equilibrium.[9]

As 'A Clear Signal' implies, all signs, whether those sent by the Irish Bishops, or by Gerry Adams, whether the written word of the Irish constitution, or Muldoon's own written 'signal' are 'open to interpretation'. Nontheless, given its self-conscious 'clarity' it is perhaps not surprising that this poem was not included in *The Annals of Chile*. Instead a less clear, even 'murky' signal appears in the poem 'Cows', in which the border is crossed in secret, and where we find the poet nearly run down by a cattle-truck while taking an evening country walk with a friend:

> Even as we speak, there's a smoker's cough
> from behind the whitethorn hedge: we stop dead in our tracks;
> a distant tingle of water into a trough.
> [...]
> This must be the same truck whose tail-lights burn
> so dimly, as if caked with dirt,
> three or four hundred yards along the boreen
>
> (a diminutive form of the Gaelic *Bothar*, 'a road',
> from *bo*, 'a cow', and *thar*
> meaning, in this case, something like 'athwart',
>
> 'boreen' has entered English 'through the air'
> despite the protestations of the O.E.D.):
> why, though, should one tail-light flash and flare,
>
> then flicker-fade

---

[9] As always with Muldoon however, there is another level of allusion here, for 'widdershins' and 'deasil' are also words used by Yeats and Joyce. This is more than a nod at the power of Ireland's two great writers, however, for in some sense they represent alternative currents in Irish culture: one Protestant, and one Catholic. Moreover both terms are introduced in connection with women. Yeats uses 'withershins' to describe the power of Lady Gregory to create an intellectual community in 'Coole Park, 1929'. Significantly he imagines a form of progress and enlightenment which is not linear or teleological: 'The intellectual sweetness of those lines/That cut through time or cross it withershins'. As I will discuss below Joyce employs the term 'deasil' in connection with childbirth in 'Oxen of the Sun'.

> to an after-image of tourmaline
> set in a dark part-jasper or -jade?

This dim signal flashes on a dim or diminutive road, at any rate off the main thoroughfare. The implication is that this is a so-called 'unapproved road' across the border, like the imaginative crossing or dissolution of borders in 'Brazil'. Here the signal turns from the red of the tail-light, to green (though not Irish emerald but tourmaline – the poor man's emerald). What are we to make of this subtle morse code – does it symbolise a substitution of the Red hand of Ulster for the green flag? Or are we to assume that the night-time paramilitary manoeuvres evidenced by the cattle truck are responsible for the 'gangrene' of 'A Clear Signal'? The poem asks us repeatedly to interpret the signs it contains, but it also makes it impossible to do so by offering so many, and so many contradictory ones.

As is fitting for a companion poem to 'A Clear Signal', 'Cows' evinces a similar concern with the links between sectarian violence in the North of Ireland, and the repression of women throughout the island. The next section of the poem offers a surreal vision of lowing cattle, seemingly suffering from a terminal illness: 'That smoker's cough again: it triggers off from drumlin/to drumlin an emphysemantiphon/of cows.' This is surely the sound of death – the rattle of lung cancer and the inability to breathe. How are we to read this signal? There is an allusion here to the story of the slaughter of Hyperion's sacred cattle in *The Odyssey*. This crime against the gods is punished by the death of Odysseus' men – and the omen which they are sent is the bellowing of the dead cattle. This episode is taken up by Joyce in 'The Oxen of the Sun' to denote a crime against fertility (in contraception or abortion), with the cows as symbols of femininity and procreation. Muldoon in turn seems to be suggesting that the crimes in Ireland are not only those of the 'tit-for-tat murders' in the North, but also the crimes against women throughout the island.

Not that it is at all easy to say what 'Cows' 'means', and Muldoon makes the most of this poetic indeterminacy. His own etymological, allegorical interpretations mock our interpretative strategies. It's as if he is saying, you're looking for signs to interpret, so I'll give you them, I'll even interpret them for you. The final section of the poem takes his characteristic practice of offering ironic 'advice' on how to read the poem to an extreme:

> *Oscaraboscarabinary*: a twin, entwined, a tree, a tuareg;
> a double dung-beetle; a plain
> and simple hi-firingparty; anoff-the-back-of-a-lorry drogue?
>
> Enough of Colette and Celine, Celine and Paul Celan:
> enough of whether Nabokov
> taught at Wellesley or Wesleyan.
>
> Now let us talk of slaughter and the slain,
> the helicopter gun-ship, the mighty Kalashnikov:
> let's rest for a while in a place where a cow has lain.

Instead of deep meaning and significance, Muldoon takes the portmanteau word he has created, and dissects it. Rather than any more fundamental or significant connection, the twin here is the twinning word, a double dung-beetle surely refers to the two 'scarab's hidden in the word. We might take this to signify life emerging out of death, but the poem moves on through association to other warnings and portents. Muldoon is trying to have it it both ways – offering omens, and at the same time undercutting any import they may have by revealing their arbitrary character. Moreover this exploration of the process of interpretation turns the end of the poem into a problem to be solved. The final sestet suggest that the warnings are about a recurrence of violence. Forget etymology, the poem seems to say, forget arbitrary distinctions, forget the literary, and start to think about life and death in the real world. Yet these distinction (between Celine and Celan for example) are important. They are not merely linguistic games – indeed such differences are a matter of life and death. Similarly the rhyme words of the closing tercet undercut the seemingly heartfelt and direct message at the end of the poem. For the final lines, while echoing the penultimate tercet, also circle back through rhyme to the beginning of the poem. The implication is that the 'serious' talk of 'the mighty Kalshnikov' is itself interrupted by the diseased bellowing of the cows: 'Even as we speak, there's a smoker's cough/from behind the whitethorn hedge.'[10]

---

[10] This interpetation is strengthened by the fact that the poem's beginning 'in medias res' is signalled by an asterisk, so that we can't be sure where the narrative starts.

'Relief'

'Cows' ends by questioning the opposition between formal linguistic or literary distinctions and the expression of 'true' emotion. One of the implications here is that it is wrong to think of formal control as the antithesis of authentic feeling – indeed that tightly controlled and 'conventional' forms may be the best vehicle for the expression of overwhelming feeling. In keeping with this, Muldoon utilises some of the most 'worked' literary forms (derived from Dante and the troubadours) such as terza rima, the villanelle and the sestina, in poems which express grief and loss as well as love and grace. At times Muldoon's adoption of formal mechanisms of control seems almost obsessive: 'Incantata', the long poem written in memory of his former lover Mary Farl Powers, not only adapts the eight line stanza Yeats uses in 'In Memory of Major Robert Gregory', but at the same time uses the rhyme words of the long poem 'Yarrow', in the order in which they first appear in the poem (and then, from the middle of the poem, the rhyme words are repeated in reverse).[11]

Despite the expansiveness and more direct autobiographical, intimate tone of 'Yarrow' then, the formal complexity of the work remains. Moreover the poem is as weighted with literary allusions as 'Madoc – A Mystery'. The poem is set up as a retrospective on the previous thirty years of Muldoon's life, with the winter of 1962–3 as a central focus, (although 1972, and 1982 are also important dates in the poem, dominated by the figure S- – for sex? – as much as by his parents). The many literary allusions are 'motivated' in the main by the boy's reading, (although the references to film and cinema going are equally important, and some literary references, for example to Sylvia Plath, are links drawn in retrospect, since she died in the winter of 1962). Among the child's favourite authors are Rider Haggard, Sir Walter Scott and Alexander Dumas (the conflict between supporters of the Cardinal and those of the Queen in *The Three Musketeers* serves as an imaginative displacement for battles between the U.D.A. and the I.R.B., with the spy Milady Clark playing a central role on both sides of the ideological divide!)

---

[11] As Muldoon has pointed out, Yeats had borrowed the stanza from Abraham Cowley's 'On the death of Mr. William Hervey'. The complexity of the moving poem 'Incantata' deserves an essay to itself, and I will not attempt an interpretation here.

Then there are the narratives which enable specific imaginative connections with South America, or the South Seas: *Treasure Island*; Jack Shaefer's *Shane* (the story of an enigmatic cowboy of Irish extraction, and a battle over land); the story of one man's ride from south to north America with his horses Mancho and Gato, *Tschiffley's Ride*. And despite the child Muldoon's antipathy to the old Irish texts foisted on him by his mother in the poem, his world is seen through the lens of medieval epics such as *The Song of Roland*, Malory's *Morte d'Arthur*, and (to add a Portuguese flavour) Camoes' *The Lusiads*. The confusions generated by this plethora of films and books are compounded by the child's fluid boundaries between reality and fiction. He is forever transforming into adventurers in his imagination, as well confusing the members of his own family with characters from adventure fiction, epic and medieval romance.

In contrast with this rich detailing of the imaginative life of the child and adolescent, the poem is marked by an abiding sense of having been abandoned. In a very specific way the poem 'Yarrow' is about confusion and loss. One of the central 'events' of the poem is the child Muldoon's loss of a carbon slip order for seeds from the local seed merchant, Tohill's of the Moy. The loss of this slip, leads to further 'slip' as the child misremembers or confuses 'marrow' with 'yarrow', leading to an imagined agricultural nightmare in which he purchases not the vegetable seed needed for his father's market gardening, but the flowering plant, and the rogue seedlings then seed themselves across the arable land. The poem plays with the structure of a bildungsroman, or narrative of development, except that development never seems to occur. The child certainly loses innocence, he 'slips' from innocence into knowledge (imaged in the deshabilee white slip of his dreams). But at the same time as charting a loss of childhood innocence (and hence a 'gain' in knowledge), the poem also circles around the loss of 'secret' knowledge. In part the poem is confusing because something is missing.[12] As Muldoon puts it at the very end of the poem, something has been 'forgotten or disavowed' – would the regaining of this repressed element clear up the confusion, make things fit, tender relief?

The poem begins with a premonition of loss:

---

[12] One might compare here Muldoon's previous formal experimentation with bits 'missing' in *The Wishbone*.

> Little by little it dawned on us that the row
> of kale would shortly be overwhelmed by these pink
> and cream blooms, that all of us
>
> would be overwhelmed, that even if my da
> were to lose an arm
> or a leg to the fly-wheel
>
> of a combine and be laid out on a tarp
> in a pool of blood and oil
> and my ma were to make one of her increasingly rare
>
> appeals to some higher power, some *Deo*
> this or that, all would be swept away by the stream
> that fanned across the land.

The pink and cream blooms are those of the plant yarrow.[13] Muldoon has said that the poem was sparked off by a visit to his childhood home in March 1992, when he saw that, due to the changes which had been done to the house, all, bar the pampas grass in the garden in which he had lain to read as a child, *had* been swept away. The poem presents a kind of imagined foreknowledge of change (due in reality to the death of his parents and the sale of their house). Yet these lines are puzzling; for why should Muldoon suggest that all would be overwhelmed 'even if' his father were to suffer some terrible accident? The implication is that the mother's invocation of a 'deus ex machina' will fail – this is to be an epic without gods. An additional irony is latent in the fact that being overwhelmed by yarrow is (in part) a positive, healing thing. Yarrow, or *Achillea Millefolium*, is a curative herb, a plant for stopping nose-bleeds – so called because Achilles is reputed to have discovered its use.

As Muldoon has stated, this is a poem 'about a deep-seated hurt'. Violence and bloody noses are associated with the father in the poem, but at issue is not only the violence done to the father, but the violence done by hm. The father in this poem appears in a very different light to the picture of him in Muldoon's earlier work, such as 'The Coney' or 'Cauliflowers'. The tenderness and protectiveness of the son towards the father noticeable in these poems is displaced. The association of the father with violence occurs firstly through

[13] Although 'Yarrow' also suggests, by implication of the word 'stream', the river Yarrow in the border country of Scotland. The Scottish connection is marked by the presence of Scott and Stevenson in the poem, but the title also recalls Wordsworth's poems about Yarrow (where he was taken by Scott).

the mutation *of* rhyming words. Towards the beginning of 'Yarrow', the father is 'quiet, almost craven'; this transmutes into Arthur Cravan, the 'poet-pugilist' lover of Mina Loy; this in turn transmutes into 'Artillutteur Ecrivain' – fighter writer; and then 'Agravain' – the fearful character from *Morte d'Arthur*.

The father's awful strength is first of all revealed in relation to the time when

> my da took a turf-spade to poleaxe
>
> one of McParland's poley cows
> that had run amuck on our spread,
> bringing it to its knees by dint of a wallop so great
>
> it must have ruptured a major vein,
> such was the spout
> of, like, blood that hit him full in the face.   (63)

Later the blood on his face is his own when, in a manner reminiscent of Popeye, he loses his temper with his Protestant neighbour: 'all I remember was the sudden rush/of blood from his nose, a rush of blood and snatters.' (77) Throughout most of the long poem however, the father is associated with a violence the son fears will be turned against himself. His father becomes 'Agravain of the Hard Hand', or even 'Agravyn a la Dure Mayn' – a fearful character who disapproves of the child's reading. (107/108) As he travels on his imaginative journeys in and around the barn, his actions are punctuated by overheard statements, admonitions, and interruptions which mount up, to a final 'capture' by the father.

> 'I'd as lief,'
> Agravain was muttering, 'I'd as lief you'd stay and help me redd
> up after the bluestone barrels are scoured.'

The main task in the winter of 1962–3 seems to be that of spraying the potatoes (like the imagined take over by the yarrow, various larva have already infested the leaves of other vegetables).[14] A version of the mother remonstrates against the child's unwillingness to help on the farm: 'What in under heaven/did we do to deserve you, taking off like that, in a U-boat,/when you knew rightly the

---

[14] One literary reference for the poem is surely Patrick Kavanagh's lyric 'Spraying the Potatoes'.

spuds needed sprayed?', (154) (although perhaps foolishly she fails to listen to her son's explanation: 'I've just lit the fuse/on a cannon'). The final sections of the poem focuses on the child's fear of the father:

> again and again I wedge my trusty Camoens
> in the barn-door to keep it ajar
>
> lest Agravyn a la Dure Mayn
> mistake me for Ladon or some apple-butt dragon
> and come after me; even now I hear his shuffle-saunter
>
> through the yard, his slapping the bib
> of his overalls; even now he stops by the cattle-crush
> from which the peers and paladins would set out on their
>   forays.

In the next poem the powerful Emir catches up with the Muldoon character in the barn: 'again and again they cry out,/"Open, Sesame."' The results of his 'mitching' are confusedly in evidence in the final tornada, where the young Muldoon character is to be found leaving the farm 'with my arms crossed, click, under my armpits'. The click is one of remembrance or sudden realization – his hands, which earlier in the poem were 'bandaged' with talc, are in pain from the beating with a 'freshly-peeled willow-switch' (This is a punishment we are familiar with from Muldoon's early poem 'Anseo' – where it was administered to another boy by the school-teacher, who also happened to be Muldoon's mother).

While a painful past is in evidence here, the poem also enacts the search for a cure for this hurt. Throughout the volume the search for 'relief' is central; a recurring motif is the need for mitigation or assuagement, whether the turn to herbal remedies for cancer in 'Incantata', the relief which S- seeks in drugs, the mother's reliance on God, or the desire for nutmeg (ravensara) as sweetener of the endless repetetive diet of the Irish – which is imaged not only as the gruel or porridge the mother eats in hospital, but also as conflict and violence.

The end of the poem suggests that the overflowing of the 'stream' of curative Yarrow will only ever be about to happen 'shortly', that the healing of loss and confusion has not taken place in the past and cannot take place in the present. As the poem repeatedly reminds us, time is not a healer but the devourer of everything.

> In a conventional tornada, the strains of her 'Che, sera sera'
> or 'the Harp That Once' would transport me back
> to a bath resplendent with yarrow
>
> (it's really a sink set on breeze- or cinder-blocks):
> then I might be delivered
> from the rail's monotonous 'alack,alack';
>
> in a conventional envoy, her voice would be ever
> soft, gentle and low
> and the chrism of milfoil might over-
>
> flow
> as the great wheel
> came full circle . . .

The desire here is to go back in order to be 'delivered', but time (whatever will be, will be/ The Harp that once) doesn't work like that. Instead the poet is left trying to figure out an 'indecipherable code', abandoned with 'no more relief, no more respite' than he experienced in the past.

Tempus Edax Rerum

Superficially 'Yarrow' seems to suggest that we are entirely boxed in by our past, so that a return to the past in order to find some understanding of our present situation, and therefore some possibility of a different future, is doomed to failure. Muldoon clearly believes that the contours of Irishness need to be rethought or reconceptualised in the present world order, but the repetitive and circling structure of *The Annals of Chile* suggests that a way out of the cycle of familial and national violence is not easy to find. It may, however, be possible to think of the overall 'message' of *Annals* in another way, and in the remainder of this essay I want to consider the formal structure of the poetry in more detail, in order to suggest that possibilities for the future may indeed be found in the repetition or reproduction of the past.

The sonnet 'Twice' serves as a useful introduction to these concerns. The poem returns us to Muldoon's childhood, to the terrible winter 1962/63 when (as Muldoon says in connection with Plath's death, in 'Yarrow'), 'It seemed as though ice burned, and was but the more ice.':

> It was so cold last night the water in the barrel grew a sod
> of water: I asked Taggart and McAnespie to come over
> and we sawed and sawed
> for half an hour until, using a crowbar as a lever
>
> in the way Archimedes always said
> would shift the balance, we were somehow able to manoevre
> out and, finally, stand on its side
> in the snow that fifteen- or eighteen-inch thick manhole cover:

'Twice', like 'Brazil' and 'Cows' is a poem about the underworld (accessed through the manhole cover), about turning against the sun, and rejecting the gods. The poem was published soon after the scandal surrounding Bishop of Galway, Eamonn Casey's fathering of a son. The two characters who aid the speaker of the poem are ironically named Taggart (son of the priest, sagart), and McAnespie (son of the bishop). Linear time and succession is associated here with paternity (in constrast with the feminine 'cutting across time' noted in the use of the terms 'widdershins' and 'deasil'). The Archimedean point is the point at which a lever is balanced, as well as the point at which perspective is reached, (a point then which depends on the distance of the observer). This measured perspective is disturbed in the final sestet however:

> that 'manhole cover' was surely no more ice
> than are McAnespie and Taggart still of this earth
> when I squinnied through it I saw 'Lefty' Clery, 'An Ciotach',
>
> grinning from both ends of the school photograph,
> having jooked behind the three-deep rest of us to meet the Kodak's
> leisurely pan; 'Two places at once, was it, or one place twice?'

Taggart and McAnespie are not 'still of this earth', perhaps because they are sons of god the father? Lefty Clery is a left-handed cleric, therefore ill-omened, on the side of the devil and the underworld. It is he who disrupts the spatial co-ordinates of perspective and linearity by introducing the element of time and therefore repetition. For the still school photograph is also a moving picture, which can contain the same elements twice.

In 'Twice' the boundaries of time are disrupted, just as space is contracted in 'Brazil'. Muldoon has signalled the importance to him when he was writing *The Annals of Chile*, of Jorge-Luis Borges's essay 'A New Refutation of Time'. In this essay Borges recounts a moment on a street in Buenos Aires which he experienced exactly as though it were occuring thirty years previously. On the basis of this experience of exact repetition across time and space, he maintains that time in the sense of succession does not exist (for if there is exact repetition then the experience is the *same* one, and not a recollection). 'Twice', like 'Yarrow' also returns to 30 years previously, exploring not only the concepts of linear or cyclical time, but also slyly suggesting the possibilities of divine or devilishly inspired filial 'succession' within the church.

There is a lot to be said about the meditation on questions of sameness and difference in *The Annals*; throughout the volume Muldoon seems to be asking when is repetition not repetition, or reproduction, but the same. In 'Yarrow' repetition occurs at every conceivable level, linguistic and narratological. There is firstly the repetition of syllables: oscaraboscarabinary, lillibullabies, expiapiaratory. Then the repetition of phrases (often themselves having to do with time) 'That was the year', 'again and again', 'even now', 'all I remember'. Characters in the narrative repeat themselves: 'But to the girdle do the gods,/she repeats, but to the girdle do the gods inherit'. Even Muldoon's supper 'repeats on him'. Reference is made too to literary 'repetitions': Plath's 'poppies in July, October poppies.' The narrative device of the poem is that of memory, in which events can be endlessly repeated. Memory itself is triggered by the VCR (the 'background' to Muldoon's recollections) on which films, and sections of films, can be not only 'remade' but also replayed: 'that same poor elk or eland/dragged down by a boblink;/the umpteenth *Broken Arrow*'. Muldoon seems to be taking the notion of a 'remake' of his own work to extreme ends in this book, where not only are familiar concerns taken up again, but images and phrases from earlier poems are worked into the book. The quoof, Brazil, immrama, pampas-grass, mile-long cadillac, cauliflowers, all make a (re)appearance. This is of course fitting for a work which is structured as an obsessive return to events of the past, for the images of childhood which may have figured in earlier poems are still embedded in the imagination of the child and adult. Moreover 'Yarrow' is a meditation on the whole of his life, of which the poems are a part.

Repetition is also a *formal* principle in 'Yarrow' as a whole. Muldoon has decribed the structure of the poem as 'twelve, intercut, exploded sestinas'.[15] This is a little misleading in fact since the twelve rhymed poems which form the templates of the sequence are not strictly sestinas, since they contain twelve, nine or six lines (there are thus 90 rhyme word in all, over a poem of more than 1000 lines). To take the poem of twelve lines which opens the sequence, this is repeated seventeen times, but with six variations on the order of the rhymes (as in a conventional sestina). The six variations themselves form a pattern throughout the poem, as at certain points the rhyme scheme is repeated without alteration. In addition there are six variations on the order of the end-rhymes, so that these quartets also rhyme with one another at intervals, and they do so in a pattern, though a pattern which (significantly) seems to break down at moments. The order of the 'sestinas' could perhaps best be described as a pattern with random elements, as increasingly the poems repeat preceding forms, often rhyming perfectly with the preceding poem (rather than offering a variation on the order of the rhyme words). After the central poem, which rhymes with the first, the sequence reproduces the exact order of all the preceding seventy five poem forms in reverse, ending with a variation on the first poem. One could argue that the pattern needs a sense of 'randomness' because it has do to with memory, and an obsessive return to the subject.

The random pattern allows Muldoon to introduce even more elements of repetition into the structure of the conventional sestina. Poems rhyme with one another across the sequence, and in addition to repeating rhyme words, corresponding poems very often repeat phrases and whole lines of poetry. The repetition of rhyme words creates perfect rhyme; it is surely the end of rhyme. However, Muldoon modifies this structure by allowing the rhyme words to mutate gradually across the sequence. In this way the rhyme helps the reader work out the associations, for example between craven, cravan, ecrivain, and agravain. In addition such repetition allows connections to be made between different moments, as a picture of a life is built up through fragments.

The fact of variation in repetition is crucial for an understanding of the poem – is Muldoon always returning to the 'same' (in which case time and succession, as Borges suggests, is rendered null), or does the poem progress through subtle variation? As I have argued, the tornado at the end of 'Yarrow', which repeats all 90 end rhymes

---

[15] Are there twelve because there are twelve months in the year?

of the poem, suggests that 'progress' cannot take place because something is 'missing'. The nutmeg or sweetener, which would offer some 'relief' to the violent cycle of familial and national history has been lost. On the other hand the form of the poem itself, which does progress despite always having to use the same elements, the same raw materials, suggests the possibility of a different future. Importantly however, that future is not imagined in terms of linear succession (the son supplanting the father) but as the circling, tentative, 'homing' flight of birds which, like Yeats's swallows, can cut through time.

Conclusion

I have suggested that *The Annals of Chile* can be read as an exploration of the possibilities for change and progress, both within the framework of a search for political equality and democracy in Ireland, (and by analogy with Chile, the Americas too), and the framework of personal, familial – and specifically paternal – relations. The volume's search for 'relief' from the endless repetitive diet of violence, grief and loss in both state and family is in part thematic and in part formal. Muldoon, now resident in America, asks whether 'translation' from the old world to the new can make a difference, yet it is clear that what he is searching for is not a new focus or a new subject-matter, but a means to create something new out of the same materials – his memories of his childhood, Irish literature and Irish history. Hence this volume has the feel of a meditation on or a 'summing up' of Muldoon's work to date, as he considers the possibilities of ways not to reproduce, but to create, out of the same past. As I have discussed, the parallels he draws with Irishmen of the past who have 'translated' themselves from the Northern to the Southern hemisphere, and from the old world to the new, have a far from equivocal meaning. For while Bernardo O'Higgins, the champion of enlightenment and republicanism in Chile, may stand as a corrective or a balance to the repressive measures taken by O'Reilly in the service of Catholic, Royalist Spain, the subsequent violent and anti-democratic history of Chile suggests that the consequences of enlightened 'progress' may be ambivalent. While the analogy here with the history of Ireland's failed eighteenth century republican revolution is obvious, the fact that in Chile's more recent history terror and violence are most clearly associated with the state apparatus, rather than insurgent forces, may give us pause to wonder about the precise significance of Muldoon's analogy between the history of the two countries. Moreover, state terror in Chile has been supported by the political and economic power of North America, so that again, as I discussed in relation to 'A Clear Signal', the question of where 'backwardness' and political 'progress' may be found within the global system is a moot one.

If geopolitics is revealed as a particularly difficult science in this work, as superficially different political cultures turn out to have many disturbing similarities, so too is the attempt to differentiate past, present and future. On an autobiographical level, this merging of events in the writer's life clearly corresponds to his struggles with memory, and his battle to find a way, having once acknowledged aspects of his own past, not to repeat or reproduce them in the future. Such a preoccupation has resonances in terms of his reflections on the (im)possibility of progress within the political realm too.

Yet I have suggested that despite the underlying bleakness of much of this volume (imaged for example by the cyclical structure of 'Cows' which always leads us back to the beginning, confounding any attempt at progress or understanding through dialogue), the overall 'message' of the work may offer a corrective to this view. At one simple, but nonetheless important level, progress does occur throughout the volume. Out of the 90 end-rhymes in 'Yarrow' come more than 1000 lines of poetry in which at least the beginnings of a new self-understanding seems to be attained. Moreover, those same end-rhymes provide the structure for the elegy 'Incantata'. The subject of this poem too is the search for relief – for a way of living in the knowledge of mortality, and for a balm to heal the dying body. In his obsessive use of repetition surely Muldoon is suggesting that poetic 'incantation', rythmic repetition, may be one way to ward off evil, and to find a deeper kind of understanding, so that it may be possible to at least face the future. (Similarly Yeats's lines 'that cut through time' are as much lines of poety as the circling flight of the swallows). If this language of loss, growth and understanding through poetry seems very 'unMuldoonian', it should be stressed that this is not presented without irony on Muldoon's part – indeed the humour of the work can be read as the element of 'relief', the sweetener which offers the possibility of change or diversion from sameness.

In addition to humour, diversion can also be interpreted as an alternative to linear progression, or succession from father to son.

Succession never takes place without being routed through a woman, of course, but part of Muldoon's point is that aspects of sexuality which do not fit in with the patriarchal story have effectively been denied, in Ireland as elsewhere. At issue here is sexual pleasure and eroticism, and nonreproductive sex in general, but also the crimes against fertility associated with the word 'deasil'. Rather than abortion and contraception, Muldoon associated such crimes with Catholicism and the Southern State's control of the female reproductive body – imaged perhaps in the devouring uterine and breast cancer in 'Yarrow' and 'Incantata'. Alternatives to paternal succession are symbolised by the woman in the volume, though their forms of diversion differ widely – from the mother's stock of classical and literary allusions, to the erotic and drug-induced diversions offered by S-. But implicitly the most significant diversion, or alternative route towards progress may be found in the birth of Muldoon's daughter. The gestation and gradual physical realisation of the baby throughout *The Prince of the Quotidian* and *The Annals of Chile*, is paralleled by the father's own emotional realisation that in the child reproduction is always also creation of something different. Given Muldoon's past record, of course, it is unlikely that he intends to present this rather wholesome, organic metaphor without irony.

Licence[1]

ROBERT SMITH

for Michal ben-Naftali Berkowitz

SAY WE CHOOSE not to take poetry and politics for granted as given terms. Say then that these cannot ingenuously be picked up and combined in a 'poetry and politics', a conjunction created to stimulate academic discourse. Accordingly say that nor can poetry and politics simply decouple after encountering each other, free to go their separate ways once more.

Will these things be granted? Will they be permitted, licensed, credited? Is the hypothesis sanctioned for now?

But instead of indulging the obscurantist or possessive motive – or the polemical one – which would sequester poetry and/or politics from the opportune combination of 'poetry and politics', let the relation between them be revealed as more than just casual or academic. There may be an essential, more necessary relation between them, though its form may be negative. An *essential* trait of the poetic might be its capacity to turn away from politics either when it chooses or when it has no choice but to do so. To head off confusion at the outset: I do *not* mean to imply that poetry and politics are mutually exclusive, on the contrary, but only that the poetic *can always* – even if, in the instance, it does not – annul its engagement with the political. That is, even if a given poem embraces and unfolds the political in every theme and reference, and even if its poetic form actively seeks to insinuate political position, or even if such a final abjuring of politics itself contains political implications, the poetic perhaps is what reserves the right to revert to the strictly a-political – and even though 'the strictly a-political' be but a fantasm ... In its core, poetry's relation to politics would be one of apotropaic closeness. This defensive gesture would therefore constitute a part of poetry's essence. But this essence would be conceived less as a quiddity than as an inalienable power. Despite the fact that 'defensive gesture' suggests poetry's having

---

[1] The present essay represents the slightly modified version of a lecture first given at Bucharest University on 3 April, 1995.

existence as an ego, we are heading with this hypothesis away from the possibility of either poetry or politics as free-standing substances, egoic or otherwise. (The movement away itself affords a second-level defence.) For if the negative relation to the political defines it, then poetry as such cannot exist independent of that relation, and the reverse argument could be applied from the side of politics. If this is so, the hypothesis we are entertaining is one of right, the right of denegation, more than one of substance. And such a hypothesis would be a far cry from either (1) the historicism that frames poetry in a political context and insists positivistically how poetry is 'determined' by it, supposing poetry essentially explicable in terms of the social phenomenon it presents; or (2) the flipside: the pastoral occlusiveness which wants to shelter poetry from the imagined dangers of politics, the lamb from the wolf. *Both* positions remain 'aesthetic' in so far as they approach poetry as a delimitable object, a thing with a given border – aesthetic, that is, in terms of what an art object requires as a condition, before it can be received phenomenally. Before it can be viewed or addressed, and as a condition of the horizon of its experience, it must be presented, put forward, delimited from what surrounds it – framed.

Through and through it could be a matter of licence. What would we be treating of, were we to understand poetry according to this capacity it has, the one which makes it poetic (though in a nonaesthetic sense), and not according its phenomenon as an object? We would be treating a poetico-political negative energy, a chemistry of potential revulsion each from each, a law of the fission into distinct elements, poetry and politics. – And this would seem to lead straight back to the comfort of 'poetry and politics', a given poet say, set against his or her political background. But a dissymmetry in the energetic relation of poetry to politics leaves a complication, and suppresses their ideal separability. For while we conjecture that the poetic be a *right* of acceding to the a-political, rights can be recognised as such only from the political side of the equation. The right to turn away from politics is not a right among others. So we should have to consider where and how poetry receives its licence, so to speak, in this hyper-juridical moment. Presumably in turning away the poetic cuts itself off from political forms of authorisation, preferring to take the law into its own hands, winning its licence privately from itself, endorsing *de jure* its latitude from political licensing and jurisdiction? I employ the term 'licence' to serve as more than a pun, and what the phrase 'poetic licence' designates now reaches beyond the local abuse of language in poems, to cover the terrain of poetic possibility, affirming: that is poetic which licenses itself; which receives its authority from within in a *causa sui* manner; which may negotatiate immediately its own freedom.

The complication condenses further. This freedom contributing an inaugural and structurally irrevocable part of its 'essence', poetry is bound to it as to a *de jure* characteristic. Therefore, poetry will have created a new law or duty for itself despite being, or because of being, free from the law and duty in their political forms. And anyway, what would a poetry be that were entirely free from the obligation to its own freedom, its freedom of speech? Regardless of constraints imposed by genre, social ambience, author's 'life-world' – and even censorship – poetry, in order to be *poetic* (in order for this to retain distinct value), will have to be concerned with this its own 'difficult liberty'. Any turning away from politics must result in deeper contact with ethics, in an irony analogous to that of atheism having to occupy itself more than theism with God, as Nietzsche remarked. The realm of the poetic would appear ethical in this precise sense of there where legal certainty, as meted through political channels, has yet to be obtained or has been surpassed. It, poetry, emerges as the ground of the responsibility for its own freedom. – But there persists the question of how this responsibility is actually licensed, or whether self-licensing has any authority, which we shall come back to.

In this fashion, we will have deferred a more conventional, which is to say more readily licensed, literary-critical beginning that takes up poetry and politics as phenomenologically given and thematically compatible, opening up instead along an ethical axis. But to return briefly to the beginning, since the right to speak obliquely and hypothetically (that is, ultimately, *ethically*, as I shall try to argue) involves a question of the authority required to set up new discourse and what criteria have to be met: the beginning was itself 'poetic' if it did not straight away slip into the maelstrom of 'poetry and politics' as an academic theme, or if it provoked a tension over academic protocol. It held back from the journalistic momentum otherwise sweeping us towards 'poetry and politics'. By doing so, it ran the risk of augmenting the desire for just such a 'poetry and politics' all the more. It stood still. But standing still cannot be neutral, we can now say, for this 'poetic' already figures in two relations of responsibility – the relation to what it turns away from, and the relation to its own freedom or isolation.

In other words, to think about poetry and politics we might do better to hold back from treating them as an academic theme, on the grounds that the academic may itself be a form of the politics that poetry veers away from. Yet all the while grows the desire to hear the politics that treats of substance and theme get under way, a desire which as a third responsibility now urges itself upon poetry. What is the relationship between poetry and the desire it redoubles in others for the daily discourse of (academic) politics? If it does redouble that desire, isn't poetry responsible a third time? Is one responsible for the desire one creates in others? And what of the jealousy aroused by this privileged freedom of poetry, this specialised supplement or favouritism within the democratic universal of *our* 'polis', the academy? Does poetry have an academic place?

A further, subjacent principle flickers in these questions. (The first principle was that the poetic can always denegate the political.) A further right of overriding belongs to the poetic as a power to paralyse the momentum towards the daily discourse. In more literary-critical terms, the capacity the poetic might have to denegate or abjure the political corresponds to its native ability to subdue or exclude narrative. As in the previous case of poetry and politics, poetry and narrative are not strangers, they can and do co-exist, coalesce, in texts, but poetry can as much estrange narrative as espouse it. Poetry can always eschew narrative and present only image, even if it does not, and even if when it does a narrative may be inferred from the image by a reader. The association with narrative does no damage to it as poetry. At the same time poetry can always halt its narrative simply to look, to see and not to hear for a moment. Even 'narrative poetry' keeps this power within it, and even the most archaic, as a kind of dehiscence that does not need to be made present.

Fairly contained though this principle may appear, it, like the one it subtends, telegraphs toward a logical absurdity. For the principle that poetry *can always* cut narrative short will not be impaired even if poetry *never does*. – So the hypothesis becomes valid *because* it need never be tested! At least apparently. But this needs to be thought through. In fact, we can reclaim this apparent absurdity for reason by translating the thought behind it: namely, that an unexercised right remains a right. And put like this, it may become less absurd. Not only is an unexercised right still a right, but the very notion of right implies the reserving of right as potential. The twin rights held by poetry do not as rights differ from, say, a right to vote. My right to vote does not mean I have to keep on voting, nor that I waive it if I do not vote at all (any right that is removed from one who does not exercise it must be a tacit form of coercion or force, as opposed to the generosity or indulgence that lies at the heart of the concept of right); similarly, nor does poetry have continuously, or *ever*, to exercise its twin rights of denegation (of politics and of narrative). Rights are powers, their potency consists in their potentiality, or the essential possibility of their non-use *as much as* of their use. That is what makes of them a right rather than a truth or essence (an immanence within the thing).

It also makes my hypothesis about poetry an 'ethical' rather than philosophical hypothesis, i.e., a matter of power, or politics, rather than of truth and essence. It is irrelevant that the hypothesis cannot be tested, for that would be to work within the field of philosophical essentialism and quiddity (we would be testing a truth), whereas for now what concerns us is hypothesis as licence, authority, capacity, power, right. What weighs in this case is that my hypothesis be granted, not that it be true, and how the machinery of recognition operates. I try to overcome poetically a political-academic discourse of objective or essentialist description in order to be more sympathetic to the poetic. Which hardly benefits me with greater *subjective* surety, the return to self having been cordoned off, in the sense that the present discourse may remain unlicensed. Rather one tries to occupy this hypothetic dimension between poetry and politics, and in doing so confuse our discourse with that of the poetic: a practice which, moreover, for Derrida at least, would count as another principle, indeed, of the poetic. (Derrida, 1991, 221–37)

And my hypothesis says that poetry itself may be a matter of licence, licensed to license itself in a moment of pure transfer of power without agency, at the vanishing point of positive law. This sublime transfer constitutes its right and as such something that can remain hidden within it, but not so as to be *preserved* within it, for a right does not require active preservation by the one who owns it; if it is truly a right – and we are speaking in a transcendental register – it requires no protection. Rather, the right recedes beyond protection and neither need be nor can be secured by its owner. The poetic 'owns' the right, has licence to, turn away from the political, but strictly the right cannot belong to it as a property and cannot therefore be assimilated to the essence of the poetic. Put in the form of a paradox this means that the essential trait of freedom which characterises the poetic does not form part of the latter's essence. From its reserve, the licence works only as *actio in distans*. The poetic cannot properly belong to itself in so far as it is powerless to assume fully its own character, this character residing in a right which lies by definition outside incorporation. And the gap between itself and itself takes the form of a negative bind to the political. In turning away from the political, poetry does not return to itself, at least not quite. It starts back in that direction but fails every time to come home into its essence.

This is perhaps the sense in which poetry is free. It is free from itself as an essential self. Its return to self being foreclosed, its freedom is however more one of exile than of rational liberty or critical dissent. Set forth by an ethical impulse, it goes simply on the wrong path to expect a return to its essence. Metaphysically speaking, the poetic expresses the intimate disjunction between ethics and essence (ontology).

Hence 'difficult liberty' or negative freedom. The poetic may be the ground of responsibility for its own freedom, but is incapable of grounding that freedom in its essence. Consequently, there will needs be some other authority or licensing agency which will recognise the right to freedom *as* a right, as opposed to the way in which the poetic itself wants to recognise it: in ontological terms, i.e., as the (privative) relation to its own essence. But where can such an authority be found once poetry has turned away from politics as the dispensing machine of laws and rights? How does its right to freedom become a *right* to freedom, as opposed to the mere form of its own inaccessible essence? Only through a further impossible necessity, or 'aporia'. Only through the extreme attempt at positing that authority for itself, whereby the right can be recognised ethically as a right – for a right must be recognised, the licence must be stamped. A residual and indissoluble *will* to legislative authority informs the poetic perhaps, even as it turns away from such authority in its political forms, even as it comes into its own through the sloughing off of necessity.

The poetic, it seems, springs from this chicane of freedom and necessity, the ethical frustration of its own essence which liberates it, and the ambiguous will to an authority to recognise its free status (it 'knows' that laws are only posited, rights only granted, that the will infects all authority). It quivers in this medial role: suspended essence, suspended authority, both of them yet furnishing the 'telos' of the poetic. It takes definition from what it cannot have, not as lack or 'desire', but as what sustains its apotropaic relation to the political, burning up no more than a ribbon of political oxygen.

The example of John Milton might activate these arguments which for all their universalism could be charged with presupposing a freedom specifically 'Protestant' in origin. Consider: the poetic becomes the ground of responsibility for its own freedom. A break from established sanctioning releases the poetic towards its largely private and individual – one might say idiomatic – relation to itself. The Protestant is self-licensing in a similar sense, capable of generating for him- or herself a freedom nonetheless yoked to responsibility as self-discipline. From this perspective, ethics would symbolically 'begin' with the Reformation, established ecclesiastical authority rolled back to allow for the manifold self-colloquy taking place in the penumbra of doctrinal law. I stress the multiplicitous and idiomatic nature of this ethical 'beginning', for ethical anxiety contracts upon the loss of unequivocal authority, catalysing 'points of view'. (There is no ethics without opinions; in the nature of ethics lies a deferral of consensus.) These points of view contend in a milieu that is at first social, for access to the political is now mediated necessarily by 'individuals' (always more than one). A kind of category shift occurs, whereby in principle the political gives itself for thought nowhere but through social data. For Milton, social variety must be acknowledged for there to be any serious political thought at all. More radically, political thought as genuinely political thought depends upon that variety, because 'society' steps forward as an uncircumventible premiss of politics. A non-social politics cannot be a politics, remaining 'cloistered' and 'unbreathed', in words evocative of prelatical reserve and corruption.[2] One could even say that it is too private, and permit ourselves thus to distinguish it from Protestant privacy. Protestant privacy and individualism are, paradoxically, social, and have to be so. A related and more demanding paradox is that a turning away from politics offers the sole authentic means of political engagement, that a certain poetic refusal of politics makes their apotropaic link all the closer, for politics as a divorcibly non-social element will have foregone its validity.

---

[2] In the famous words of Milton's tract on freedom of speech and the licence to print: 'I cannot praise a fugitive and cloistered virtue, that never sallies out and sees her adversary, but slinks out of the race, where that immortal garland is to be run for, not without dust and heat.' (Milton, 1931, 311)

To the extent that it opens into this 'free' Protestant dimension, Milton's poetry is inherently social, and especially when the more idiomatic, or singular – society realises itself in the specificity of its parts. The idiom is what has been breathed, the privacy that, being social, has been exercised and taken out of the cloister. 'That which purifies us is trial':[3] its virtue is virtuous only in so far as it has been tested, hence Milton's taking over of Romance motifs in *Comus*, for example, to establish in the figure of the Lady the durable kind of virtue as the right kind, exposed in an extreme way to outside forces in their contrapuntal animadversions. The corybantic brigade of Comus represents licence in the second sense, as licentiousness, the feral freedom that has failed to bind itself in an ethically meaningful way. Authentic freedom binds *itself*, the Lady's chastity nicely emblematic of the logic, and can be at best parodied by the fetters used by Comus to ensnare her which are external and belated, according to the text's generally Pauline system of values (authentic and internal versus external and inauthentic). The true bonds of (chaste) religion are contrasted with those of magic whose predilection for change and transformation, for psychic alchemy, puts it at once on the other side of virtue as unchanging durability. Her steadfastness pre-empts the fastening by which the psychopomp leashes her. He binds her so as to unbind her, but in vain:

> *Comus.* Nay lady sit; if I but wave this wand,
> Your nerves are all chained up in alabaster,
> And you a statue, or as Daphne was
> Root-bound, that fled Apollo,
> *Lady.*   Fool, do not boast,
> Thou canst not touch the freedom of my mind
> With all thy charms, although this corporal rind,
> Thou hast immanacled, while heaven sees good.[4]

The quality of freedom as self-binding and resistance to change has developed from the poetic relation to the political. As such, it involves the allied principle of the paralysis of narrative. Poetically, the Lady resists the 'spell'. She resists the magical (and, by association, Catholic) psychogogic power of what is related, the intoxicating sequence and rhythm of what continues as it changes, and changes as it continues, all in a hierophantic motion of prestidigi-

---
[3] Ibid., 311.
[4] Milton, 1971, 209, ll. 658–64.

tation, gesture, ritual. Her duty is to turn the weaving of the spell, the wave of insinuation, to glass – to draw upon the image by which her saviour Sabrina is identified, 'under the glassy, cool, translucent wave' (line 860). The poetic must glassify the stream of rhetorical undulations (as liquid as those of the serpent in *Paradise lost*). But the rhetoric is essential, as the means for testing poetical virtue and as the means too, by extension, of stoking it up, drawing it away from the deathly archivism of hermetic privacy; stalking it, rhetoric draws virtue away from rhetoric. The hermetics of (Catholic) rhetoric antagonistically sustain in a dialectics the openness of (Protestant) free poetry, displaying thereby the difference between political-hermetic *hermeneutics* and socially vented *interpretation*. The paradox this time is that the poetic overcomes the esoteric authority of Hermes and Circe by itself tending toward the elliptical, shrinking the elaborations paraded by rhetoric to a pinpoint of resistance, meeting the rolling eyes with the fixed eye of conscience, stilling the knowing narrative: silence is the mark of poetry as virtue. But poetry must never assume this mark, and seal its lips, for then it has given over proving itself in the test. Poetry risks becoming its opposite, wants to lay down the law. In the terms used above, it matters that poetry never embrace the ethical trait that defines it: silence. Being ethical, poetry cannot become what it is. It speaks, and this causes an ambiguous doubling of the politics it refrains from. A legislative will resurges, as the will to virtue.

The example not only illustrates the argument about the 'ethical turn', the Lady withstanding poetically, that is ethically, the rhetorico-politics of Comus, but at the same time the argument about the need for poetry's licence to be countersigned has begun to be borne out. This time, the register changes to the soteriological. The legislative will to virtue needs some kind of secondary endorsement. Sabrina seems to perform this function, just as the 'one greater' in *Paradise lost* and *Paradise regained*, seems to perform it too – Jesus Christ. Both saviours are the countersignatories of freedom, the embodiment of ethical, as opposed to politico-legal, authority. They figure the will of those whom they save, those with 'free will' (the Lady, Adam and Eve), in that they are projected forward typologically as what will come to the rescue. In other words, the saviour figures by default embody the future, or deferred redemption (redemption-as-deferred), because their existence is contingent upon the intention towards them, the will to their authority, on the part of those who are temporarily lost. That would be the *will* in free will, and it is the condition of the free extrapolation in poetry of its own history. The characteristics of this will, then, are less psychological than ethical in the sense of quasi-legal, with poetry as the very bordering upon this medial habitus and the unavoidable courting of authority albeit in altered form; equally, the characteristics of such a will are historical in a typological sense, with the freedom of free will obliged to forge a world-historical dimension.

One might even say that the problematics of Milton's libertarian cosmology derive from just the semantic *contre-sens* in the word 'licence' as it simultaneously denotes (1) token of authorised permission, and (2) epicurean permissiveness. Milton's project would then be to regulate the paralogism, making sure that licence never shades into licence even though it is licensed by the dialectical relation with it, and so on ('lest I should be condemned of introducing licence, while I oppose licensing', Milton, 1931, 298). One cannot really tell whether this is 'mere word-play' or something far more serious, especially given that for Milton the realm of interpretation not only coextends, but coincides genetically, with that of society as the realm of political reality. Moreover, once one simply decides the meaning of a given word, or arbitrates for it in a perhaps Hobbesian style, one runs the risk of relapsing into a form of hermetic-hermeneutic authority – the imposition of meaning, authority as diktat, sovereign certitude, etc. So 'linguistic' or 'semantic' intractabilities must be respected, and precisely because they are not linguistic or semantic, i.e., are not subject to hermeneutic arbitration. Language is not 'language' in Milton, just as poetry, in a quite rigorous sense, is not poetry but freedom. Freedom as the ethical suspension of essence 'is' what poetry 'is', which supports the point that the language of poetry cannot be fixed essentially, and not only in cases of ambiguity (though we are a long way from a celebration of 'polysemy').

From Milton's point of view, at least in his 'idealist' phase, the regulation required occurs bottom-up, as it were, from the *res publica*. Coming full circle, then: republicanism offers the means by which language can become 'language' again and take on public, intersubjective semantic *meaning*, as opposed to being appropriated by code and shibboleth. It tolerates the co-existence of alternatives. Meaning flourishes as an ethical phenomenon; language means in an authentic sense because unconstrained by 'meaning' in the hermeneutic-semantic-essential way, and the massive manoeuvre in

Milton's poetry from the unit of the word to that of the sentence serves the ethical programme. Meaning emerges from the republic of the sentence made dialectical so as not to be sententious. Time is built into it as the historicity that accompanies ethical diversity in its dramaturgy, and as the attenuated sentence which relays a series of 'semantic' choices.

Constituted of freedom, poetry entails the making ethical of politics. The case of Milton suggests that politics is merely political unless pulled onto this ethical turning-board. The ethical turn 'realises' politics not in its essence, but in its more serious and ongoing irradicating in social concern. (One could even describe it in Kleinian terms, as the transition from paranoid to depressive position.) Essence is false freedom, 'bad consciousness'. For when politics is merely political it is *merely* its essential self, has not itself been exposed to the 'test' that makes of it a considerable, responsible, 'real', if ambiguous form of life. The poetic turn away from politics revolves the political deeper into itself, overcoming the supplementarity of politics and the profit the very supplementarity offers to those in power. The *inclusiveness* of the political-poetic world, the inhibition against either's splitting off from the other, marks the Miltonic point of view almost as if it were a kind of Spinozism. What sets it off against Spinoza, however, is the uncollapsibly typological dimension created by free will, which implants time and creation and the creator God into the system.

The presence of Spinoza reminds us that our hypothesis may presuppose a particular Protestant notion of freedom rather than 'a' Jewish one, say; though it is not Spinoza so much as Emmanuel Levinas who has been at the back of the remarks made so far. The phrase 'difficult liberty', for instance, is his: *Difficile liberté* was published in Paris in 1963; and the thesis that ethics takes precedence over ontology (essence) is of Levinasian sort. I would like to gather up the arguments so far and add them to a broadly Levinasian view of ethics to try and see, albeit nebulously, how 'determining' the question of religion and race may be for the relation of poetry to politics.

Now, Milton's typology would compute an England-as-Israel, through the world-historical resumption of ethical reality. A kind of Anglo-Zionism pulses in the work, save that the relation to the law has been ethicised in such a way as to allow for a pneumatic (Pauline) relation to it. The law folds into the human, rather than the human having 'judaically' to graduate towards the law: judaically, that is, if one has the right to manipulate such stereotypes, narrowing the band that separates one from the law while maintaining the law's otherness, striving to *live by it* in a near literal sense, and by the repetition of it. The law for Milton, by contrast, can be streamed, as it fans out into social minds. Though regulative, it can be carried individually, the innate movability, i.e. spirituality, being what in general had allowed its destination to be transferred from the land of Moses to England. Analogously, the migration from Eden eastwards proves the law's movability (the Protestant 'church' may be set up anywhere). Consequently England as a 'place' is both authentic ground of ethical reality, in so far as it receives the spirit which by nature has motion and authenticates any ground upon which it destines itself; but inauthentic for the selfsame reason – the unimpeachable mobility of the law mocks the power of any ground to ground it. Again, the ethical (spirit) cannot come into its (authentic) essence. The Protestant can inhale the spirit on condition that it be breathed out again, so the legitimating power of the spirit abides at a 'judaic' distance after all, which induces a need for greater discipline. How else *can* spirit retain law as law, as what in principle must overrun unique incorporation? The exigency of the law, the law of law, as it were – is that it pertain to more than one, that it proscribe the exemptability and indivisibility of the subject, and of the nation. The law cuts subject and nation open.

At the bottom of spirit lies a futurality keeping its ethicity alive, making of its essence an unfinished glissade towards itself. The Protestant engages this futurality, and a typological poetry submits its form to shaping by it. Memory need only be schematic, the freedom of the will being taken up rather with the prospect of reformation. And although the Protestant form of freedom may restitute in some wise a 'judaic' relation to the law, as the law's recurrent unmasterability (masterable law is not law), it would be on this question of memory, of past and future, that the distinction Protestant/ Jewish might taughten again. Later on I shall try to show why the stereotypes I am using are even more profoundly problematic than at first sight they appear, but to continue for now to hypothesise in this vein: it is not that Jewish free will does not exist, plainly, but the Jewish harping back to and living by the law differs greatly from free will in the generally Christian but specifically Protestant dimension – which is willful, futural, exploratory, having been barred from the return to self. That prohibition dates from the Fall. The gate closes behind you, you are outside. The plain that yawns ahead is the same, retrospectively speaking, for Christian and Jew alike who are as yet undivided, except that Christian redemption changes the weight of memory on the Christian's head. One must be alive to the time scheme here. Memory *will have been* at a greater remove for the Christian because of the retrospective credit afforded by redemption, and this removal, for the Protestant in particular, provides a sanction for greater 'free will' in the now more expressly political sense. To Reformers, Catholicism had been tending to become unfree, and merely political, and to that extent un-Christian, its memory clogged rather with recent changes of office, than deepening into its authentic typological dimension which gives its freedom space. Memory *can* become subliminal, typological, of a different order – and for the Protestant, it ought to. It will have been taken care of, as it were, by subliminally channelled typological reassurance, by the promise of Christ, which releases Protestant freedom as individualism and responsibility among individuals; whereas the sublimation of memory for the Jew would represent a kind of irresponsibility, or failure of testimony. Jewish memory would unlock this anamnesis, bringing the ideal form of the law into everyday life, incapable of putting it in reserve (to this extent Spinoza remains thoroughly 'Jewish'). The Jew does not require that the ways of God be justified in quite the same, rhetorical, way, even if s/he might in an existential one. That requirement is more likely in the belated, rationalist, republican Protestant realm, where God can be discussed as an ideal political object, and objectified as a set of principles, precisely because He has been bracketed out to the subliminal dimension.

The rationalist realm is slightly too expedient, as it were, where the ethical relations between individuals are contingent upon their individualism (which works as an a priori even though it too has a provenance of its own in divine law), rather than upon a more irrefutable, 'earlier' ground. There arises the need for consensual self-regulation, and poetry itself can become a didactic form of such regulation: its homiletic impulse, for Milton at least, cannot be stifled. Justification has jurisdiction for a neighbour, to put it baldly. And on these lines, Hobbesian thought would offer merely the most neurotic expression of this ambiguity in Protestant freedom. But for Levinas, we know that ethical relations do not wait upon an individualism, for the relation to the other precedes rationalist individualism; that testimony cannot be speculated into an anamnesic archive; that place may be exploded long before the logic of spirit breaks it up; that politics involves a more profound resistance of the temptation of place.[5] So what are the implications for poetry and politics?

Again, politics is not politics if merely political; if preoccupied with its own 'polis', the jealous guarding of its place, the substitution of custodians, esoteric repetition. For Levinas politics is incipiently 'pagan' on account of such reductiveness. It reduces itself to a nationalism of sorts, the stupefied adherence to roots, land, territory, place. This is one reason why a truly ethical politics will encourage the technological advance that transects locality, breaks the ground up. Maintaining the openness is the role of (ethical) politics, rupturing the ground violently for the sake of a 'pacifism'.

The role of poetry might become exemplary for such a politics, and here I want to speak less about Levinas, in fact, than about another poet – Paul Celan.[6] If the right to turn away from politics keeps politics alive, and if this right characterises the poetic (without us being able, however, to derive an essence of the poetic from it), the liberty thus won – and it is a difficult liberty – looks nevertheless as if it will vary according to 'Protestant' or 'Jew'. Protestant liberty appears to enter into a rationalistic network framed by typological structures of thought, making of memory a superstructure, so to speak; while it would be a nonsense to suggest that there is no Jewish typology or typologism, the relation to memory appears however to be more – to keep with the metaphor – infrastructural. There is a judaic elision of anamnesis, as it were, while unelided anamnesis represents the Platonism underpinning the Pauline typology underpinning Milton. It would be just as nonsensical to take Celan simply for a 'Jewish' poet: one thing linking him to Levinas is a perception of the Jew as being essentially in a state of crisis with regard to being a Jew, uncertainly Jewish.

The uncertainty makes the need for close memory all the more pressing, a need for bearing witness perhaps rather than memory (see Felman, 1992). The Holocaust is the 'political' event throwing its shadow forward in this case, Nazi politics pre-eminently pursuing the reduction of the political to the guardianship and extension of

---

[5] To the reader less familiar with such Levinasian themes, may I recommend *The Levinas reader* (Levinas, 1989)?
[6] I have benefited greatly from discussion of Celan and related themes here pursued, with members of the *'Schibboleth'* reading group in Oxford. My debt to that text in particular will also be evident (Derrida, 1986).

place, roots, exterminating whatever is homeless in regard to it, incapable of tolerating either the ethical interval from the essential self or the turning away from politics which refuses to comply in the essentialist stare ahead. Nazism would be the epitome of politics as such. According to our hypothesis, a 'pure' politics would be non-spiritual, essentialistic – the politics of Nazism exemplifies it, which sacrifices spirit to blood. Being 'spiritual', though in different ways, both Protestant and Jew ideally converge in their opposition to this politics of blood-without-spirit. In a sense, the Protestant spiritualism detailed above conforms to a Jewish position because its logic concludes that the spirit can never land once and for all, that redemption can never be won unequivocally and essentially; one might win it ethically, of course, however, but this is the common root of anxiety, for the winning becomes a matter of value, not fact. Redemption is always 'to-come', even after Christian redemption, because its form is spiritual. Poetry might be the audacious occupation of this quasi-substantial realm, whether we call it Protestant or Jewish. It would embrace spiritual uncertainty, or rather spirit as the very mode of uncertainty, producing anxiety for itself the most salient symptom of which would be the minimal but basal will to certainty, authority, legitimation (a will which may be managed with more or less responsibility). Poetry perhaps becomes a means of thinking this 'paranoid' politics, by turning away from it in an apparently hermetic gesture that would in fact be an opening up of politics from its super-essentialism, its genetic closedness, its blood jealousy, its territorial sway. Poetry would represent a chance for depriving extreme politics of its terrifying closure by racism.

I believe this dystopic, ethically political and testimonial form of poetry to be acute in Celan. It is not just Celan's biography – that of mid-European peripatetism and linguistic mutation – which imbues it, but also the fact of a poetry that is everywhere outside of itself, translated into an exterior with no corresponding nucleus. One can read these 'facts' as the mark of a *Deus absconditus est* or as the priority of translation over home-truth, so to speak, though the two perhaps amount to the same. His poetry is politically grave precisely because the borders of the 'polis' are brought more into focus in the turning away from them. The hermetism of Celan's poetry stems perhaps from such an apotropaics, and the language of his famous address *The meridian* has everything to do with this postponed meeting up with oneself in a moment of political *Aufhebung* (Celan, 1986).

Accompanying the 'moment' of turning away from politics is a rarefaction of the idiom, a qualification of the generality of political forms of law, indeed of law in general. At the same time, however, the law must overspill absolute containment by an individual, as argued above, for it to remain *law* and for ethicity to obtain some requisite authenticity. Otherwise, it looks dangerously like political coding – poetry resembles what it's least like. If now I turn to an 'example' of Celan's writing, as, first, an example of Celan, and, second, as an example of the poetry of a 'Jew', even an 'uncertain' Jew, the spuriousness of doing so must therefore be borne in mind. The poem I choose (as though a choice system were in place allowing one to generalise indifferently from specific instances) is the following:[7]

LES GLOBES

In den verfahrenen Augen – lies da:

die Sonnen-, die Herzbahnen, das
sausend-schöne Umsonst.
Die Tode und alles
aus ihnen Geborene. Die
Geschlechterkette,
die hier bestattet liegt und
die hier noch hängt, im Äther,
Abgründe säumend. Aller
Gesichter Schrift, in die sich
schwirrender Wortsand gebohrt – Kleinewiges,
Silben.

Alles,
das Schwerste noch, war
flügge, nichts
hielt zurück.

Micheal Hamburger's translation has:

LES GLOBES

In the eyes all awry read there:

the sun, the heart orbits, the
whizzing, lovely In Vain.

[7] Celan, 1988, 210–11.

> The deaths and all that
> to which they gave birth. The
> chain of generations
> that lies buried here and
> hangs there still, in the aether,
> and borders abysses. All the script
> on those faces into which
> whirring word-sand drilled itself – tiny eternities,
> syllables.
>
> All things,
> even the heaviest, were
> fledged, nothing
> held back.

The turning away from politics runs the risk of becoming a victim of politics, or, the witness is a martyr, as the word 'martyr' itself suggests. All things were fledged, the gaze of this witness is absolute, nothing can remain outside of it, there is not a political selection as to what one will see and what one will turn a blind eye to. Because of this the poetic gaze begins to lose focus, whereas the political, the merely and terrifyingly political, can select selectively, it can select examples, cases and races: it can select both the master and the slave race. But the idiomatic, poetic regard is absolute or total in a manner quite different from a totalitarianism: 'Alles'. This 'Alles', being a totality, cannot be grounded, can be buried only to the extent that it still hangs here, bifurcating vision ('Die / Geschlechterkette, / die hier bestattet liegt und / die hier noch hängt'). Such is the generality of this 'Alles', included thoroughly in the chain of generations, 'die Geschlechterkette', 'immanently'. The generations form a *chain*, they are historical in a linked and unbroken way, they have a future and a past which is that of this absolute 'Alles' that contains moments of the absolutely specific figured in tiny eternities. These are not specific essences or examples so much as moments of this intra-responsible generational chain which may be of greater magnitude than a politics could master or extinguish, except that Nazism comes close to doing just that. It comes close to taking generational death away from selected races and replacing it with political death, i.e. the death that selects who will die in the face of the fact that all will.

This 'Alles' and its cognates ('Les Globes', 'Die Tode und alles', 'Aller / Gesichter Schrift') give the colour of a poetry indigestible to a politics that can control all things in only a striated, aristocratic, selective and esoteric fashion, through a logic of the example and of representation. One cannot *represent* an All. Perhaps Celan's is a non-representational poetry of the All, or of the immanence too intractable for 'mere' politics to comprehend – provoking, fatally, the jealousy of politics, its licence to kill. Poetry treats even the most intractable, 'das Schwerste noch'. It takes on this absolute responsibility toward what it cannot represent – 'Alles' – and suffers the burden of repletion. Witnessing cannot represent, but it can swear, to agitate the etymology of 'Schwerste'; it makes an oath, a hypothetic or ethical bond, that is. The impossibility of grounded representation, expressed as we have noted in the paradox of internment while hanging there still, is figured in the breaking up of the ground, 'literally': the abysses, 'Abgründe', which are bordered. One turns away from politics towards these abysses that lie in the direction of essence which can be approached in two ways: (1) as witness to the abyss opening as the hell into which non-essential ethical humans are thrown (victims); (2) through the poetico-ethical unavailing attempt to come into one's essence. This latter could be seen as a kind of primary masochism such that what Nazism does, as an extreme politics, is to anticipate that masochism and kill off what, because it was human, was on the way to dying anyway and dying not least because it had never, because it was ethical, achieved birth into its own essence – it never quite 'lived'. Nazism kills the non-essence that was *already* suffering from the ethical inaccessibility to essence; it adds political suffering to ethical suffering; it activates and performs godlessness in front of those who are already godless. The two abysses engulf one another, deepen and become this supra-total 'Alles'.

If it may be granted that the abysses 'figure' this all, then a poetics is implicated too in the ethical question. The relation of ground to figure, literal to metaphorical, passes through an ethical warp making essentialist recuperation unfeasible unless it regress to the political will or aggression which decides what stands for what. To regress is to lapse back from the ethical modernity of poetry, a modernity which charges poetry with the swelling burden of memory that the future tenders. Precisely because it cannot comprehend it, poetry maintains the 'Alles' through the chain of generations. This leads to an inevitable ellipsis in poetic figuration, the eyes awry, where figure and ground co-exist without translating each other, both suspension and internment – but this is the ethical ellipsis of having too much to say and respond to ('eyes talked into / blindness'),[8] rather than that of code as based on identity politics . . . Might the 'Umsonst', the 'In Vain', be interpreted in this way? The deaths are in vain if they cannot receive adequate representation, yet to represent and classify points to the province of terror. The loss of clear representation makes way for what Celan names 'truth': 'A RUMBLING: truth / itself has appeared / among humankind / in the very thick of their / flurrying metaphors.'[9]

So as not to let this poem be merely representative, I quote also the following lines:

> O diese Wege, galaktisch,
> o diese Stunde, die uns
> die Nächte herüberwog in
> die Last unsrer Namen. Es ist,
> ich weiß es, nicht wahr,
> daß wir lebten, es ging
> blind nur ein Atem zwischen
> Dort und Nicht-da und Zuweilen,
> kometenhaft schwirrte ein Aug
> auf Erloschenes zu, in den Schluchten,
> da, wo's verglühte, stand
> zitzenprächtig die Zeit,
> an der schon empor- und hinab-
> und hinwegwuchs, was
> ist oder war oder sein wird –,

> O these ways, galactic,
> O this hour, that weighed
> nights over for us into
> the burden of our names. It is,
> I know, not true
> that we lived, there moved,
> blindly, no more than a breath between
> there and not-there, and at times
> our eyes whirred comet-like
> toward things extinguished, in chasms,
> and where they had burnt out,
> splendid with teats, stood Time

---

[8] 'Zur Blindheit über- / redete Augen.' The opening lines of 'Tübingen, Jänner', ibid., 176.

[9] 'EIN DRÖHNEN: es ist / die Wahrheit selbst / unter die Menschen / getreten, / mitten ins / Metapherngestöber.', ibid., 263.

on which already grew up
and down and away all that
is or was or will be –,[10]

– I read this figure of mitochondrial time as an inflection of the 'Alles' (it is reminiscent in its unassailable pregnancy of Picasso's *She-goat*). Her galactic milk, like the spermatic elements in other of Celan's poems, affords a moment of simultaneous prolepsis and analepsis, the generational chain exposed to view, standing in the thick of historical forms expressed in their tendency, that of surreal acceleration: 'kometenhaft schwirrte ein Aug / auf Erloschenes zu'. A narrative arrest impinges itself, but again rather one of swollenness and repletion, too much time for narrative to order. History and non-history co-exist, as the poetic turns away from the 'real' while taking it with it, the next stanza reading:

ich weiß,
ich weiß und du weißt, wir wußten,
wir wußten nicht, wir
waren ja da und nicht dort,
und zuweilen, wenn
nur das Nichts zwischen uns stand, fanden
wir ganz zueinander.

I know,
I know and you know, we knew,
we did not know, we
were there, after all, and not there
and at times when
only the void stood between us we got
all the way to each other.

Schematically, the poetic concerns itself with a 'both . . . and . . .' structure more than with an 'either/or': 'wir / waren ja da und nicht dort'. Free to assume a greater burden of responsibility, a 'pregnancy', generational repletion, it loses access to an essential saying of itself. It makes the political more difficult for itself, and increases the stakes of ethical responsibility, 'und zuweilen, wenn / nur das Nichts zwischen uns stand, fanden / wir ganz zueinander'.

[10] *Ibid.*, 158–9.

Reprise

The examples of Milton and Celan offer no proof, given that we are working in a hypothetic register that can remain indifferent to testing. So the examples are examples without an axiom or law which they might have demonstrated, in effect. At a second level, the concept of giving examples itself can be seen to be caught up in political questions. The poetic cuts itself off from exemplification: there must be something about it which resists classification and licensing, in order to remain poetic; on the other hand, it goes too far, brings politics inadvertently into itself, and suffers from an over-burdening that has the same result – too much matter for one to excise an exemplary moment. This causes an 'ethical density', as it were, that is played out across two times, historical and elliptical. In Milton the temporal splitting works as tension between silence and justification; in Celan as tension between galactic time and wartime. The tension makes these different times almost indistinguishable from each other, and it touches the heart of politics which is also its own heart. On the question of memory, there appears to be some difference between Milton and Celan. There perhaps is no redemptive typology to free up of memory in Celan. The 'will' that remains, however, remains one of address, as in Milton: an apostrophe to the enigmatic 'you' of Celan's poetry. The 'you' accompanies Celan in a more intimate way than the saviours accompany personas in Milton, but it is still an essentially apostrophic figure. Could the poetic ever do without this address, that is, overcome the will and pathos that is carried over in its departure from the political? More simply, can it do without recognition?

There appears to be no choice but to take poetry and politics together as linked in an ethically primary manner. Above all this means going beyond taking either as separable and given.

References

Celan, P., 1986, *Collected prose*, trans. Waldrop, R., Manchester, Carcanet.
———, 1988, *Poems of Paul Celan*, trans. Hamburger, M., London, Anvil Press Poetry.
Derrida, J., 1986, *Schibboleth: pour Paul Celan*, Paris, Galilée.
———, 1991, *Between the blinds: a Derrida reader*, ed. Kamuf, P., Hemel Hempstead, Harvester Wheatsheaf.

Felman, S., 1992, *Testimony: crises of witnessing in literature, psychoanalysis, and history*, New York and London, Routledge.
Levinas., E., 1989, *The Levinas reader*, ed. Hand, S., Oxford, Basil Blackwell.
Milton, J., 1931, *The works of John Milton*, vol. 4, New York, Columbia University Press.
———, 1971, *Complete shorter poems*, ed. Carey, J., London and New York, Longman.

Notes on Contributors

Helen Groth is Lecturer in Nineteenth and Twentieth Century Literature in the School of English and American Studies at the University of Exeter. She has just completed a doctorate on Victorian women's poetry at King's College, Cambridge. Forthcoming publications include articles on Victorian women's devotional poetry and scientific narrative in Victorian women's poetry. She is presently working on a study of representations of Victoria.

Louise Hudd is currently completing a D.Phil. on the significance of the body in the works of Charles Dickens at St John's College, Oxford.

John Lucas includes among his many books studies of Arnold Bennett, John Clare, Dickens and Elizabeth Gaskell. His other books include *English and Englishness: ideas of nationhood in English Poetry, 1688–1900; Moderns and Contemporaries; Modern English Poetry from Hardy to Hughes; The Trent Bridge Battery: The Story of the Sporting Gunns* (with Basil Haynes), and *Writing and Radicalism*, a collection of essays he has edited for Longmans. His collection of poems, *Studying Grosz on the Bus*, won the 1990 Aldeburgh Poetry Festival Prize. *Flying to Romania: A Sequence in Verse and Prose*, was published in 1992. He is publisher/editor of Shoestring Press.

Timothy Morton is Assistant Professor in English at the University of Colorado, Boulder, and author of *Shelley and the Revolution in Taste: the body and the natural world*, 1994.

Nigel Smith is a Fellow of Keble College, and Reader in English at the University of Oxford. He is the author of *Perfection Proclaimed: Language and Literature in English Radical Religion* (1989) and *Literature and Revolution 1640–1660* (1994), and several articles on early modern literature and history. He has edited the Ranter pamphlets and the *Journal* of George Fox, and is currently editing the poems of Andrew Marvell for the Longman Annotated Poets series.

Robert Smith is a Prize Fellow of All Souls College, Oxford. He published *Derrida and Autobiography* in 1995, and is a founding editor of *Angelaki*. Macmillan will publish his book on modern poetry and theory in 1997.

Clair Wills is Lecturer in English at Queen Mary and Westfield College, University of London, and author of *Improprieties: politics and sexuality in Northern Irish poetry*, 1993.